S0-BOF-206

Bible Nurture and Reader Series

From a child thou hast known
The HOLY SCRIPTURES
which are able to make
thee wise unto salvation

Bible Nurture and Reader Series

God's People Follow Him

Grade 3

Units 4, 5

Rod and Staff Publishers, Inc.
Crockett, Kentucky 41413

Telephone (606)522-4348

BIBLE NURTURE AND READER SERIES

"If you train your children carefully until they are seven years old, they are already three-quarters educated." This quote recognizes the importance of the critical early years in molding a child's life. The influences of childhood become powerful, lasting impressions.

The type of schoolbooks used certainly affects the developing appetites of our children for reading material. We will not instill in them appreciation for godly values by feeding them frivolous nonsense. We hold the Bible to be the highest guide for life and the best source of training for our children. The Bible reveals God and His will. Proverbs 9:10 says, "The fear of the Lord is the beginning of wisdom: and the knowledge of the holy is understanding." It is important that our children are exposed to truth from the beginning of their learning experience.

For the student to be exposed to the truth of God's Word only in textbooks is not sufficient to give him the very best. It is necessary for the tutor, be he parent or other teacher, to be firmly rooted in the Word of God and have the power of God's presence in his life. The Bible must be treasured as God's message to mankind. On that conviction this series is built, with the Scriptures as its very substance.

This book is designed as part of a series and will be most effective if so used. The grade three material includes the following books.

Teacher's Manual	Reading Workbook Unit 1
	Reading Workbook Unit 2
Pupil's Reader Units 1-3	Reading Workbook Unit 3
Pupil's Reader Units 4, 5	Reading Workbook Unit 4
	Reading Workbook Unit 5

Copyright, 1988

First edition, copyright 1964; revisions 1971, 1987

By
Rod and Staff Publishers, Inc.
Crockett, Kentucky 41413

Printed in U.S.A.

Code no. 88-9-03
Catalog no. 11304.3

Table of Contents

Unit 4

God's People During and After the Captivity

Lesson	Page
1. Ezekiel's Visions	10
2. Belshazzar Sees a Fearful Sight	15
3. Trouble in Babylon	20
4. Daniel in the Lions' Den	24
5. The Return to Jerusalem	28
6. Enemies Hinder the Work	32
7. The Temple Is Finished	35
8. The Story of Esther—Part 1	39
9. The Story of Esther—Part 2	42
10. The Story of Esther—Part 3	46
11. The Story of Esther—Part 4	50
12. The Story of Esther—Part 5	55
13. The Story of Esther—Part 6	59
14. Ezra Helps His People	64
15. Joy and Sorrow	67
16. The People Repent	72
17. Nehemiah's Request	75
18. Nehemiah Goes to Jerusalem	79
19. Enemies Try to Hinder the Work	82

20. Trouble in Judah 86
21. The Enemy Tries Again............................90
22. Ezra Teaches the People........................94
23. The People Obey the Law 98
24. The Prayer Continued 101
25. The People's Promises 105
26. More Work to Do 108
27. The Story of Jonah—Part 1 112
28. The Story of Jonah—Part 2 116
29. The Books of the Old Testament...........120
30. Beautiful Writings
    From the Old Testament 124

Unit 5

Stories About Jesus
From the Gospel of Luke

Lesson   Page

1. The Birth of John Is Announced..........130
2. The Birth of Jesus Is Announced 134
3. Jesus Is Born...138
4. The Early Life of Jesus and John 144
5. Jesus Is Tempted 149
6. Jesus Teaches and Heals.......................154
7. People Find Fault With Jesus 158
8. Great Teachings of Jesus 163
9. More Great Teachings of Jesus 168
10. Jesus Heals the Ruler's Servant..........171
11. Jesus Visits in Simon's Home 176
12. Jesus Calms and Heals..........................181
13. Jesus Shows His Power and Glory 187
14. Jesus Teaches the Disciples 192
15. Lessons on Love and Prayer.................198
16. Jesus Talks to the Hypocrites 203
17. Jesus Teaches His Disciples..................208
18. Jesus Heals, Warns, and Teaches.........214

19. Forgiveness and Salvation
      Bring Joy 219
20. The Rich Man and Lazarus 225
21. Jesus Teaches Great Lessons 229
22. Whom Can Jesus Help? 234
23. Zacchaeus and the Nobleman 240
24. Jesus at Jerusalem 246
25. Jesus Answers Jewish Leaders 252
26. The Passover 258
27. Jesus in Gethsemane 264
28. Jesus Is Tried and Crucified 268
29. Jesus' Death, Burial,
      and Resurrection 273
30. The Ascension 277

Unit Four

God's People During and After the Captivity

Lesson 1

Ezekiel's Visions

Ezekiel 1–3; 8; 37:1-14

Ezekiel was a prophet of God and also a priest. He lived among the Jews while they were captives in Babylon. The Lord showed Ezekiel many things in visions. One time while he was among the captives by the river Chebar, the heavens opened up. Ezekiel saw beautiful visions of God. It was so glorious to see that he fell upon his face. Then he heard a voice speaking to him.

God said to Ezekiel, "Stand upon your feet, and I will speak to you." Then the Spirit of God entered into Ezekiel and set him on his feet. The Lord said to Ezekiel, "I am sending you to speak to the people of Israel. They are a rebellious people."

Rebellious people do not like to listen to God's prophets. Such people often become angry when the prophets try to warn them. They get fierce looks on their faces and say angry words. They look as though they would like to hurt or kill the person who gives the warning. But God said to

Ezekiel, "Do not be afraid of the people. Do not be afraid of the things they say or the way they look. Listen to what I say to you. Do not be rebellious like them. Open your mouth, and eat what I give you."

Ezekiel looked to see what the Lord was giving him to eat. He saw a hand sent to him from God. In the hand was a book. This book was different from our books. It was a large sheet rolled up. The book was unrolled and spread out before Ezekiel. Words were written on the inside and on the outside of the roll. The things that were written on it were not blessings but woes. The Jews had sinned. They would need to hear words of punishment for their sins.

Again the Lord said to Ezekiel, "Eat this roll and go speak to the house of Israel."

Ezekiel did not want to rebel against the Lord by disobeying Him. So he ate the roll of the book that God gave him. In his mouth the roll tasted as sweet as honey.

Again the Lord said to Ezekiel, "The house of Israel is a rebellious house. They will tie you up so that you cannot go in and out among the people. I will make your tongue stick to the roof of your mouth so that you cannot speak to the people, because they are so rebellious. But when I speak to you, I will open your mouth so that you will be able to tell the people what I say."

One day when Ezekiel was sitting in his house with some of the elders of Judah, he had another vision. Again he saw God's glory as he had seen in visions before.

Then the Lord showed him a vision of Jerusalem. He saw terrible acts of idolatry in the gate and in the court and in the very temple of the Lord. He saw men and women and even the leaders of Israel worshiping idols and worshiping the sun. God told Ezekiel, "Because of all this terrible idolatry, I will punish Israel."

God's punishment had come to pass. Jerusalem had been conquered by enemies. Many people were killed, and some were carried off captive to other lands. Ezekiel's vision helped the people to understand that their troubles had come upon them because they had turned against the Lord.

One time the hand of the Lord was upon Ezekiel and carried him out and set him down in the middle of a valley. Ezekiel saw that this valley was full of bones. God caused Ezekiel to pass by the bones. Then Ezekiel saw that there were many bones and that they were very dry.

God said to Ezekiel, "Prophesy upon these bones. Tell them what will happen to them. Say to them, 'O you dry bones, hear the word of the Lord. This is what the Lord says to you, "Behold, I will cause breath to enter into you, and you shall live. I will lay cords on you and will cause flesh to come upon you. I will cover you with skin and put breath in you. You shall live, and you shall know that I am the Lord." '"

Ezekiel spoke to the bones as God had commanded him to do. He told them what would happen to them. As he was talking, there was a noise and a shaking. The bones were coming together! Each bone joined to the right bone to form the skeleton of a man. As Ezekiel looked, he saw the cords that hold the muscles and flesh come upon the bones. The flesh was covered with skin. But still the bones were not living people. There was no breath in them.

God said to Ezekiel, "Prophesy and speak to the wind. Say, 'This is what the Lord God says, "Come from the four winds, O breath, and breathe upon these slain that they may live." '"

As Ezekiel prophesied these words, breath came into the bodies of those who had been killed.

They lived and stood up upon their feet. They were an exceeding great army of men.

The Lord said to Ezekiel, "Son of man, these bones are the whole house of Israel. They say, 'Our bones are dried, and our hope is lost. As for us, we are cut off.' Prophesy and tell them that this is what the Lord God says, 'See, O My people, I will open your graves and cause you to come out of your graves and bring you into the land of Israel. You shall know that I am the Lord when I have opened your graves, O My people, and brought you out of them. You shall live, and I will place you in your own land. Then you shall know that I have said it, and that I have done as I said I would do.' "

Belshazzar Sees a Fearful Sight

Daniel 5:1-17

Belshazzar became king of Babylon after Nebuchadnezzar, his father. He was a proud king and worshiped other gods instead of the true God. He knew what had happened to Nebuchadnezzar his father when he became proud. But he was not wise enough to take warning.

Belshazzar had many rulers under his rule. They helped him to see that the people in his kingdom did as he commanded. These rulers were called lords. Belshazzar made a great feast to a thousand of his lords. He drank wine in their presence. While he tasted the wine, he commanded, "Bring the gold and silver vessels which Nebuchadnezzar took out of the temple at Jerusalem." Belshazzar wanted to drink wine from these beautiful dishes. He wanted his princes and wives to drink from them, too.

The golden vessels from the temple at Jerusalem were brought to the king. Belshazzar, his princes, and his wives drank wine from them.

15

They praised the gods of gold, silver, brass, iron, wood, and stone.

At that very hour, a strange thing happened. Fingers of a man's hand appeared by the candlestick. They wrote upon the plaster of the wall of the king's palace. The king saw the part of the hand that wrote. He was terrified.

No longer did the king look proud and happy. The look on his face changed to terror. His thoughts troubled him. His joints became loose, and his knees hit against each other.

The king cried aloud, "Bring in the wise men of Babylon."

The king spoke to his wise men and said, "Whoever shall read this writing and tell me the meaning of it shall be clothed with scarlet. He shall have a chain of gold about his neck and shall be the third ruler in the kingdom."

But none of the king's wise men were able to read the writing on the wall. They could not tell the king what it meant.

King Belshazzar was greatly troubled. His lords did not know what to think about this strange thing either.

Now the queen was also at this feast because the king had called for her. She said to the king,

הִנֵּה אֵל יְשׁוּעָתִי
אֶבְטַח וְלֹא אֶפְחָד

"O King, live forever. Do not let your thoughts trouble you. There is in your kingdom a man in whom is the spirit of the holy gods. In the days of Nebuchadnezzar, light, wisdom, and understanding like the wisdom of the gods was found in him. Nebuchadnezzar the king made him master over his wise men. Since an excellent spirit, and knowledge, and understanding, and interpreting of dreams were found in Daniel, let him be called. He will show the meaning."

So Daniel was brought in before the king. The king said to him, "Are you that Daniel who is of the children of the captives of Judah whom Nebuchadnezzar brought out of the land of the Jews? I have heard that the spirit of the gods is in you, and that light and understanding and excellent wisdom is found in you. The wise men have been brought before me to read this writing and tell me what it means. But they cannot tell me the meaning of it. I have heard that you can. If you can read the writing and tell me the meaning of it, you shall be clothed with scarlet. You shall have a chain of gold around your neck and shall be the third ruler in the kingdom."

Daniel answered the king, "You may keep your gifts and give your rewards to someone else.

Yet I will read the writing to you and tell you the meaning.''

Lesson 3

Trouble in Babylon

Daniel 5:18–6:9

Daniel said to King Belshazzar, "O King, the most high God gave Nebuchadnezzar a kingdom, and majesty, and glory, and honor. Because of this majesty which He gave him, everyone trembled and feared him. He killed whomever he wanted to kill and kept alive whomever he wanted to keep alive. He honored whom he wanted to honor and gave a lower place to whom he wanted to give a lower place. But when he became proud, his kingly throne and his glory were taken from him. He was driven from men. His heart was made like the beasts, and he lived with the wild donkeys. They fed him with grass as oxen are fed. His body was wet with the dew of heaven until he knew that the most high God rules in the kingdom of men and that He gives the kingdom to whom He desires to give it.

"And you, O Belshazzar, have not humbled your heart though you knew all this. You have lifted up yourself against the Lord of heaven.

20

They have brought the vessels of God's house before you, and you and your lords and wives have drunk wine from them. You have praised the gods of silver, gold, brass, iron, wood, and stone, which do not see nor hear nor know anything. You have not glorified the God who keeps you alive.

"Then was the part of the hand sent from God, and this writing was written. This is the writing: 'Mene, Mene, Tekel, Upharsin.' This is what it means: *Mene:* 'God has numbered your kingdom and brought it to an end.' *Tekel:* 'You are weighed in the balances and are found wanting.' *Peres:* 'Your kingdom is divided and given to the Medes and Persians.' "

Belshazzar commanded that Daniel be clothed with fine, kingly clothes of scarlet. He commanded that a chain of gold be put about his neck. He made it known that Daniel should be the third ruler in the kingdom.

That same night Belshazzar, the king of the Chaldeans, was killed. Darius the Median took over the kingdom. He was about sixty-two years old at this time.

King Darius set over the kingdom 120 princes to help him in the affairs of the whole kingdom. Over the 120 princes, he set three presidents. The princes were to report to the three presidents the things that went on in the kingdom and what they had done. Of the three presidents, Daniel had the highest place. The king liked Daniel better than the other presidents and princes, because he had an excellent spirit. He did not become angry or jealous. He was kind; and he did willingly, promptly, and cheerfully the work that was given him to do.

The other presidents and the princes were jealous of Daniel. They did not like that Daniel was given the highest place among them and that he was liked better than they. They tried to find fault with Daniel in the way he ruled in the kingdom. But they could not find any fault with him because he was faithful in all that he did. They could not find anything wrong in the way he did things.

Yet the men determined to get rid of Daniel. They said, "We shall not find any reason to find fault with him unless we accuse him in matters about the law of his God." They knew that Daniel would rather disobey the king than disobey God. So they worked out a plan in which Daniel would have to either disobey the king or the God to whom he prayed every day.

The princes and presidents gathered together to the king. They said to him, "King Darius, live forever. All the presidents of the kingdom, the governors, the princes, the counselors, and the captains have decided to make a royal law and a firm command that whoever shall ask anything of any God or man for thirty days, except of you, O King, shall be thrown into the den of lions. Now, O King, accept this command and sign the writing so that it cannot be changed, according to the law of the Medes and Persians, which does not change."

King Darius signed the writing, not knowing that it was intended to be a trap for Daniel. In fact, he did not know that Daniel had not helped to decide to make this royal law, for these men had lied to him. They had said that *all* the presidents of the kingdom—along with the governors, princes, counselors, and captains—had decided this.

Lesson 4

Daniel in the Lions' Den

Daniel 6:10-28

When Daniel knew that the writing was signed, he went into his house. The windows in his bedroom were opened toward the city of Jerusalem. There Daniel kneeled down and prayed, as he had always done before. Three times each day he kneeled down before this window and gave thanks to God.

The presidents and other rulers gathered together. They found Daniel praying and making requests of God, as he had always done before.

Then they went to the king. They said, "Have you not signed a commandment that every man who shall ask anything of any God or man within thirty days, except of you, O King, shall be thrown into the den of lions?"

The king answered, "The thing is true according to the law of the Medes and Persians, which does not change."

The men said, "That Daniel, who is of the children of the captives of Judah, does not pay

24

any attention to what you say, O King, or to the command that you have signed. He prays three times every day."

How sad the king was when he heard this! He was very displeased with himself. Why had he signed such a writing? He loved Daniel very much. Daniel was the most faithful worker in his kingdom. He did not want him to be killed by lions. The king tried his very best to think of some way to save Daniel. He kept thinking hard until the sun went down.

Then the men came before the king again. They said, "Know, O King, that the law of the Medes and Persians is that no law which the king signs and approves can be changed."

The king knew this. He commanded them to bring Daniel and to throw him into the den of lions. The king said to Daniel, "Your God, whom you serve all the time, He will deliver you."

The men then took Daniel and threw him into the den of lions. A stone was brought and laid upon the top of the den. The king sealed the stone so that what he had said would not be changed.

A very sad king went back to his palace. He would not eat. He could not sleep. Very early the next morning he hurried to the den of lions. There

25

at the den he cried with a very sorrowful voice, "O Daniel, servant of the living God, is your God, whom you serve all the time, able to deliver you from the lions?" Was Daniel alive? Would he be able to answer the king?

Yes, Daniel was alive. He said to the king, "O King, live forever. My God has sent His angel and has shut the lions' mouths. They have not hurt me because I am innocent and have done nothing to hurt you, O King."

How happy Darius was that Daniel was still alive! How good it was to hear his voice and to know that the lions could not hurt him! The king commanded that Daniel be taken up out of the den.

Daniel was taken up out of the den. He had no cuts, no bruises, and no scratches on him. He had not been hurt in any way, because he believed in his God.

Then the king commanded that the men who had accused Daniel should be brought. It was their turn to be cast into the den of lions—they, their children, and their wives. They did not believe in the living God to deliver them as Daniel did. Before they even reached the bottom of the den, the lions broke their bodies all to pieces.

26

King Darius then wrote to all the people of the earth. This is what he wrote:

> Peace be multiplied to you. I make a law that in every part of my kingdom men tremble and fear before the God of Daniel, for He is the living God and steadfast forever. His kingdom shall not be destroyed, and His rule shall be to the end. He delivers and rescues. He works signs and wonders in heaven and earth and has delivered Daniel from the power of the lions.

Daniel continued his work in Babylon. God was with Daniel, and things went well for him during the time that Darius was king and also while Cyrus the Persian was king after Darius.

Lesson 5

The Return to Jerusalem

Ezra 1–3

In the first year that Cyrus was king of Persia, the Lord stirred up his heart. He gave him a desire to let some of the Jews return to the land of Judah. God did this so that what He had spoken by Jeremiah the prophet would be fulfilled. God had said that He would punish the nations that took His people captive. He had promised His people that after seventy years He would bring them back to their own land.

King Cyrus made a public announcement of his desire to all the people in his kingdom. He also wrote out the announcement and sent it to all parts of his kingdom. This is what he wrote:

> The Lord God of heaven has given me all the kingdoms of the earth. He has commanded me to build Him a house at Jerusalem, which is in Judah. Who is there among you of all His people? His God be with him. Let him go to Jerusalem, which is in Judah, and build the house of the Lord God of Israel which is in Jerusalem.

28

God worked in the hearts of the people whom He wanted to go up to Jerusalem to help build the house of God. All of the people whom God moved were ready to go. The group included Zerubbabel the governor and the chief men of Judah and Benjamin. Jeshua the priest went, with other priests and Levites, and many other people. The other Jews with them who were not called to go along, gave them things to help in the building of the temple. Besides all they gave to help with the building, they also gave gold, silver, goods, and animals.

Also, King Cyrus brought out the vessels of the house of the Lord which Nebuchadnezzar had brought from Jerusalem and had put into the house of his gods. He gave these to the Jews to take along back to Jerusalem.

Many, many people returned to Jerusalem to build a new temple there. The new temple was to take the place of Solomon's temple, which King Nebuchadnezzar's captain had burned. Altogether there were 42,360 people who went, besides more than 7,000 servants and maids. Many animals were taken along with them. There were more than 700 horses, 240 mules, 435 camels, and 6,720 donkeys.

When the people arrived at Jerusalem, they built an altar to the Lord. Then they offered burnt offerings to God, as He had commanded in the Law of Moses. They also kept other feasts which were commanded in the law. They wanted to do the will of the Lord.

Much work needed to be done before they could even start to build the house of the Lord. Materials for the building of the house needed to be gathered. Cedar trees were brought from Lebanon as for the first temple which Solomon had built. The Levites who were twenty years old or older were appointed to take the lead in the building of the temple.

At last the foundation of the house of the Lord was laid. How happy the people were! The priests and the Levites sang together and gave thanks to the Lord. They praised God because He is good. His mercy endures forever for His people. All the people shouted with a great shout when they praised the Lord. They were very happy to see a new temple started. Many of the old men who had seen the first temple, wept when they saw the foundation laid.

The people could not tell the difference between the shout of joy and the noise of weeping because they shouted with a loud shout. The noise was heard a long way off.

Lesson 6

Enemies Hinder the Work

Ezra 4

The Jews who came to Jerusalem soon found out that they had enemies. In the land of Judah there were men who did not want the Jews to rebuild the temple. Though they were enemies, they pretended to be friends. They came to the leaders and chief men of the Jews. They said, "Let us build with you because we seek your God as you do, and we sacrifice to Him."

They could not fool the chief men of Israel. The leaders of Israel knew that these men were not worshipers of the true God. The leaders said to them, "You have nothing to do with us to build a house to our God. We ourselves together will build to the Lord God of Israel as Cyrus, the king of Persia, has commanded us."

Then the enemies hindered the Jews in their work. They made it hard for them to build the temple. All the years that Cyrus was king, they hindered the work. When Artaxerxes was king, the Jews' enemies wrote him a letter. In this

32

letter, they accused the Jews to the king. This is what they wrote in the letter:

Your servants, the men on this side of the river, and at such a time.

Let it be known to the king that the Jews who came up from you to us have come to Jerusalem. They are building the rebellious and the bad city. They have set up the walls of it and joined the foundations.

Let it be known to the king that if this city is built and the walls set up, they will not pay taxes to the king. Because we get help from the king's palace, it would not be right for us to see the king dishonored. For this reason we are sending a warning to the king. We suggest that you search in the book of the records of your fathers. You will find in the book of the records that this city is a rebellious city. It brings damage to kings. It is because of their rebellion long ago that this city was destroyed.

We are declaring the truth to you. If this city is built again and the walls set up, you will have no share on this side of the river.

King Artaxerxes received this letter from the Jews' enemies. It was plainly read before him. King Artaxerxes sent a letter back to the men who had written to him. This is what he wrote:

Peace, and at such a time.

The letter which you sent us has been plainly read before me. I have commanded search to be made. It is found that this city has rebelled against kings and that rebellion and riot have been found in it.

Now give the commandment to make these men stop, so that the city will not be built until I give further commandment. Be careful that you do not fail to do this. Why should the kings be hurt because of them?

When the Jews' enemies received this letter, they hurried to Jerusalem. They forced the Jews to stop working on the temple. So it was stopped until another man became king of Persia.

The Temple Is Finished

Ezra 5; 6

At last a new king reigned in Persia. His name was Darius. In the second year of his reign, the prophets Haggai and Zechariah spoke to the people. Then the work on the temple was started once more. God's prophets helped to build it.

Again men came to hinder the Jews. They asked, "Who has commanded you to build this house and to make this wall?"

By His prophets, God had commanded the Jews to build this house. And God helped them so that these men could not make them stop. They continued to build.

These men saw that they could not make the Jews stop building unless King Darius commanded them to stop. They wrote a letter to King Darius, hoping that he would command the Jews to stop. This is what was written in the letter:

Let it be known to the king that we went to

the province of Judea to the house of the great God. It is being built with great stones. Timber is being laid in the walls. The work is going fast and well for them.

We asked the older men, "Who commanded you to build this house and to make these walls?" We also asked them their names so that we could write to you the names of the chief men.

This is what they said: "We are the servants of the God of heaven and earth. We build the house that was built many years ago, which a great king of Israel built and set up. But after our fathers provoked the God of heaven to anger, He let Nebuchadnezzar, the king of Babylon, take them.

"Nebuchadnezzar destroyed this house and took the people away to Babylon.

"But in the first year of Cyrus, king of Babylon, King Cyrus commanded that this house should be built. The gold and silver which Nebuchadnezzar took out of the temple that was in Jerusalem and brought to the temple of Babylon, Cyrus took out of the temple and gave to the man whom he had made governor.

"He said to him, 'Take these vessels into the temple that is in Jerusalem. Let the house of God be built in its place.'

"We came and laid the foundation of the house of God which is in Jerusalem. Since that

36

time even until now we have been building, and still it is not finished.''

Now if it seems good to the king, let search be made in the king's treasure house at Babylon to see whether Cyrus made a command to build this house of God at Jerusalem. Let the king send and tell us his desire in this matter.

King Darius received this letter. He commanded search to be made to see if what the Jews had said was true. The records were found. It was written in the records that Cyrus the king had commanded that the house of the Lord be built.

Darius then sent word back to the men who had written to him. This is what his letter said:

Let the work of this house of God alone. Let the governor of the Jews and the elders of the Jews build this house of God in its place. Besides this, I command what you shall do to help the elders in the building of the house. Give them goods from the king and tax money for their expenses so that their work is not hindered. Do not fail to give them the animals they need for burnt offerings every day so that they can offer sacrifices of a sweet smell to the God of heaven and pray for the life of the king and his sons.

Also, I have made a command that anyone

who shall change what I say, shall have timber pulled down from his house. Let the timber be set up again and that man hanged on it. Let his house be made a dunghill. Let God destroy all kings and people who shall try to change or destroy this house of God which is at Jerusalem. I, Darius, have made a law. Let it be done with speed.

When the men received this letter, they quickly did as the king commanded them. It was very dangerous to disobey the king.

Now the Jews were helped instead of hindered. The work went well, and the temple was finished as God and King Cyrus and King Darius had commanded. The temple was dedicated to the Lord. There was great joy among the Jews.

Lesson 8

The Story of Esther

Part 1

Esther 1:1–2:4

Sometime after the temple in Jerusalem was finished, Ahasuerus became king of Persia. His throne was in Shushan the palace. King Ahasuerus reigned over a large part of the world. He had a great and glorious kingdom.

In the third year of his reign he made a feast for all his princes and servants. For six months he showed them the riches of his glorious kingdom and the honor of his majesty.

After this Ahasuerus made a feast for everyone in Shushan the palace. For seven days the people feasted in the court of the garden of the king's palace. Beautiful decorations of white, green, and blue were hung around. These decorations were fastened to silver rings and pillars of marble with cords made of fine linen and purple cloth.

The guests were given wine to drink in cups

39

of gold. There was a large amount of wine to drink, but no one was forced to drink any certain amount. They could have as much as they wanted.

Queen Vashti, the wife of King Ahasuerus, also made a feast. She invited to her feast the women in the royal house that belonged to the king.

On the seventh day of the feast, the king sent men to bring Vashti with the royal crown. He wanted to show the people her beauty. But Queen Vashti would not come at the command of the king's messengers.

King Ahasuerus burned with anger. He was much displeased that the queen would not obey him. He wanted advice to know what to do with her. Next to him in the kingdom were seven princes who were wise men. He asked them, "What shall we do with Queen Vashti according to the law, because she has not obeyed the command of the king?"

One of the princes answered, "Vashti has done wrong. She has done wrong not only to the king, but also to the princes and all the people of the kingdom. All the women will hear what Queen Vashti has done. They will think that if the queen did not obey her husband, neither will they have to obey their husbands.

"If it please the king, make a royal commandment according to the law of the Persians and Medes, which cannot be changed. Say that Vashti cannot come before the king any more. Give her place to someone better than she. When the people hear this, all the wives shall give honor to their husbands whether they are great men or not."

King Ahasuerus and the other princes were pleased with this advice. The king sent letters to all parts of his kingdom. They were written in different languages so that everyone could read his orders. He commanded that each man should rule his own house. The women were to obey their husbands.

The king now wanted to find another queen to take the place of Vashti. His servants advised him to appoint officers to go throughout the kingdom to find beautiful young women. They advised that these women be gathered together and brought to the palace of the king. Then the king could choose for himself which one he wanted for his queen.

This advice pleased the king. Many young women were brought to the king's house.

Lesson 9

The Story of Esther

Part 2

Esther 2:5–3:6

In Shushan the palace, there was a certain Jew named Mordecai. He was of the tribe of Benjamin. He had been taken away from Jerusalem and made a captive of Nebuchadnezzar, king of Babylon. This had been at the same time that Jehoiachin, king of Judah, had been taken captive.

Mordecai had a first cousin whose name was Esther. Her father and mother had died, leaving her an orphan. Because of this, Mordecai had taken Esther into his own home. He was a kind father to her. Esther was a beautiful lady. So, when many young women were brought to the king's house, Esther was among them.

The king's servant who helped to take care of the women was pleased with Esther. He showed special kindness to her. Esther and her maidens were given the best room in the house of the women. She would spend a whole year preparing to go to the king.

Every day Mordecai walked before the court of the women's house to see how Esther was getting along. He wanted to know what would happen to her.

At the end of the year, the women were called by name to go to the king. At last it was Esther's turn. The king loved Esther more than any of the other women. He set the royal crown upon her head and made her queen instead of Vashti. To celebrate, the king made a great feast to all his princes and servants and gave gifts.

The king did not know that Esther was a Jewess. Esther had not told that she was one of the Jewish people, nor had she told who her relatives were. Mordecai had commanded her not to tell. Even though she was queen, Esther still respected Mordecai as her father. She still obeyed him as she had obeyed him while she was in his home.

Mordecai sat at the king's gate. At that time two of the king's servants who kept watch at the door became very angry with King Ahasuerus. In their anger they made plans to kill the king. Mordecai found out what they were planning to do. He honored the king and did not want him to be hurt. So he told Esther what these two doorkeepers were planning to do. Then Esther let the king know about it. She gave the message to the king in Mordecai's name.

The king found out that what Mordecai had said was true. The two doorkeepers were indeed planning to kill him. He had them both hanged on a tree. An account of this was written in the king's record book.

After this the king made Haman a great man in his kingdom. He made him greater than all the other princes who were with him. All the king's servants who were in the king's gate bowed to Haman and showed great respect to him. The king had commanded them to do this.

But Mordecai would not bow to Haman nor show him great respect. The king's servants who were at the gate said to Mordecai, "Why do you disobey the king's commandment?" Day after day they spoke to Mordecai about this, but Mordecai would not bow to Haman.

At last the servants told Haman that Mordecai was not bowing to him or showing him respect. They had heard that Mordecai was a Jew, and they wanted to find out what the king would do to him.

When Haman noticed that Mordecai did not bow or show him respect, he became very angry. He had heard that Mordecai was a Jew, and he wanted Mordecai killed. But he did not think it would be enough to have only Mordecai killed. He hated all the Jews. He decided in his wicked heart that all the Jews in the kingdom of Ahasuerus should be killed.

The Story of Esther
Part 3

Esther 3:8–4:17

Haman went to the king. He wanted to get permission from the king to have all the Jews in his kingdom killed. He said to the king, "There is a certain people scattered abroad and living in all parts of your kingdom. Their laws are different from the laws of anyone else. They do not keep the king's laws. So it is not for your good to let them live. If it please the king, let it be written that they be destroyed."

The king trusted that what Haman said was true and right. He gave permission to Haman to have all the Jews killed, not knowing that this was putting the life of his beloved queen in danger. He gave Haman his ring to seal the writing so that it would be a law that could not be changed.

The king's scribes were called together. They wrote what Haman commanded them to write. They wrote to all the people who were under the rule of King Ahasuerus. They wrote it in all the different languages that were spoken in his kingdom. The letters gave orders to kill all Jews, both old and young—men, women, and little children—on the thirteenth day of the twelfth month.

Men were sent out to deliver these letters to the people. When the people read the letters, they would know that they were supposed to kill the Jews on this certain day.

As the command went out, the king and Haman sat down to drink. But the city of Shushan was perplexed. They did not know why all the Jews should be killed.

When Mordecai knew what had been done, he tore his clothes and put on sackcloth with ashes. He went to the middle of the city and cried loudly and bitterly. He came before the king's gate. But he did not go inside because no one dressed in sackcloth was allowed to go inside. In all parts of the kingdom, the Jews, like Mordecai, fasted with weeping and wailing. Many of them lay in sackcloth and ashes.

Esther's maids and servants came and told Esther what Mordecai was doing. The queen was exceedingly grieved. She sent out clothes for

47

Mordecai to wear so that he could put off his sackcloth. But Mordecai would not take the clothing that Esther sent to him.

Esther called for the king's servant whom the king had appointed to wait on her. She told him to go and see why Mordecai was dressed in sackcloth.

The servant went out to Mordecai. Mordecai told him all that had happened to him. He also gave him a copy of the writing which commanded that all the Jews be destroyed. He told him to show it to Esther. He said, "Tell Esther to go in to the king and ask him to save the lives of her people."

The servant returned and told Esther what Mordecai had said.

Esther sent the servant back to Mordecai with this message: "All the king's servants and people know that there is one law for whoever, whether man or woman, goes into the inner court to the king without being called. He will be put to death unless the king holds out the golden scepter that he may live. I have not been called to come in to the king for thirty days."

These words of Esther were told to Mordecai. He commanded to give this answer back to her:

"Do not think that you will escape in the king's house more than all the other Jews. If you will not speak to the king, some other way will be provided for the Jews. They will get help and will not be destroyed. But you and your father's house will be destroyed. Who knows but that you have come to the kingdom for such a time as this?"

After Esther got this message from Mordecai, she again sent a message back to him. She said, "Go, gather together all the Jews which are in Shushan. Fast for me. Do not eat or drink for three days, night or day. I also and my maidens will fast in the same way. Then I will go in to the king, which is not according to law. And if I perish, I perish."

When Mordecai received this message from Esther, he went his way to do as she had commanded him.

Lesson 11

The Story of Esther

Part 4

Esther 5

The Jews in Shushan gathered together. For three days they fasted, eating nothing and drinking nothing. It was a dangerous thing for Esther to go in to the king without being called. Yet Esther was willing to risk her life that her people might be saved from death. The people wanted God to save Esther's life when she went before the king. And they wanted the king to be pleased to give Esther her request to save all their lives. So they fasted for her.

Esther and her maidens also fasted. Then on the third day, Esther put on her royal clothes, the clothes that showed that she was queen. She then went and stood in the inner court of the king's house.

The king saw Esther the queen standing in the court. Would he be pleased to hold out his scepter to her and let her live? Yes. God had His

50

eyes on His people. He put it into the king's heart not to be displeased with Esther for coming without being called. The king was glad to see his queen. He showed favor to her by holding out to her the golden scepter that was in his hand. By doing this, he told her, "You do not need to die. I want to hear what you have to say."

Esther drew near to the king. She touched the top of the scepter.

King Ahasuerus said to her, "What would you like, Queen Esther? What is your request? It shall be given to you to the half of the kingdom."

Esther answered, "If it seem good to the king, let the king and Haman come this day to the banquet that I have prepared for him."

The king commanded that Haman come quickly to do as Esther had said. The king and Haman came to the banquet that Esther had prepared.

At the banquet, the king said to Esther, "What is your wish? It shall be given you. What is your request? It shall be done, even to the half of the kingdom."

Esther answered, "My request is this. If I have received favor from you, and if it please the king to give me my request, let the king and

Haman come to the banquet that I shall prepare for them tomorrow. Then I will do as the king has said.''

Haman went out that day feeling very delighted and important. He thought it was great to be invited to a banquet with the king and the queen and to be the only one who had this honor.

Then Haman saw Mordecai in the king's gate. He saw that he did not stand up or move for him. Haman was angered. He felt insulted that Mordecai did not respect such an important man as he. But Haman kept himself from doing anything mean to Mordecai at that time. He went on home.

When Haman got home, he called for his friends and his wife. He proudly told them about his great riches. He told them how the king had honored him and had given him a place higher than any other of the king's servants. He boasted, ''Yes, Esther the queen did not let anyone except me come in with the king to the banquet that she had prepared. Tomorrow also I am invited to come to her with the king.'' Then he added, ''Yet all this does me no good while I see Mordecai the Jew sitting at the king's gate.''

His wife and all his friends said to Haman,

53

"Make a gallows seventy-five feet high. Tomorrow ask the king to have Mordecai hanged on it. Then go in merrily with the king to the banquet."

This suggestion pleased Haman. He had the gallows made. It was seventy-five feet high—more than four times as high as the roof of a small house.

The Story of Esther

Part 5

Esther 6; 7

That night the king could not sleep. Because he could not sleep, he wanted someone to read to him. He commanded that the record book be brought.

The records were read to the king. In the record book was found the story of Mordecai's good deed to the king when two men were planning to kill him.

The king asked, "What honor has been done to Mordecai for this?"

The king's servants answered, "Nothing has been done for him."

"Who is in the court?" asked the king.

Now Haman had come into the outside court to speak to the king. He was going to ask him to have Mordecai hung on the gallows which he had made. The servants said to the king, "See, Haman is standing in the court."

"Let him come in," said the king. So Haman came in. The king said to him, "What shall be done to the man whom the king delights to honor?"

Haman thought to himself, "Whom would the king delight to honor more than myself?" Since Haman thought he was the one whom the king wanted to honor, he thought of something he would like to have done to himself. He said, "For the man whom the king delights to honor, let some of the king's clothes be brought. Bring the horse on which the king rides and the royal crown which is on his head. Give the horse and the clothes to one of the king's most noble princes to array the man whom the king delights to honor. Let the prince bring him on horseback through the street of the city, announcing before him, 'This is what is done to the man whom the king delights to honor.'"

The king said to Haman, "Hurry! Take the clothes and the horse as you have said. Do this to Mordecai the Jew, who sits at the king's gate. Do not let anything fail of all that you have said."

Haman took the clothes and the horse. He clothed Mordecai and brought him on horseback through the street of the city. He announced before him, "This is done to the man whom the king delights to honor."

Then Mordecai came again to the king's gate. But Haman hurried to his house, mourning with his head covered. His plan was not working. The king was delighted to honor the enemy whom Haman wanted killed. Haman told his wife and friends what had happened.

His wife and the wise men said to him, "If Mordecai is a Jew, and you have begun to fall before him, you will not have power over him. But you will surely fall before him."

While they were still talking together, the king's servants came. They hurried to take Haman to the banquet that Esther had prepared.

The king and Haman came to the banquet with Esther the queen. Then the king said to Esther, "What would you ask, Queen Esther? It shall be given you. What is your request? It shall be done, even to the half of the kingdom."

Esther answered, "If I have received your favor, O King, and if it please the king, I ask that my life and the lives of my people be spared. I and my people have been sold to be destroyed and killed. If we would have been sold for servants, I would not have said anything."

The king answered, "Who is he and where is he who is thinking in his heart to do this?"

Esther answered, "The enemy is this wicked Haman."

Now Haman was afraid before the king and queen. The king got up in great anger and went into the palace garden. Haman stood up to plead with Esther to spare his life. He could see that the king was determined to punish him.

The king returned to the banquet. As the king spoke, they covered Haman's face. One of the servants told the king about the gallows that Haman had made for Mordecai.

The king commanded his servants, "Hang Haman on the gallows."

Haman was then taken and hanged on the gallows that he had prepared for Mordecai. Then the king's anger was appeased.

Lesson 13

The Story of Esther
Part 6
Esther 8–10

That day when Haman was hanged, Mordecai came before the king because Esther had told him that Mordecai was her cousin. The king took his ring which he had taken from Haman. He gave it to Mordecai. Esther then set Mordecai over the house of Haman.

Once more Esther came before the king. Falling down at his feet, she begged him with tears to put away Haman's plan to kill all the Jews in the kingdom.

The king held out the golden scepter toward Esther. She arose and stood before him. She said, "If it please the king, and if I have found favor in his sight, and if it seem right to the king, let the letters that Haman wrote be changed. How can I bear to see the evil that shall come to my people? How can I bear to see my relatives destroyed?"

The king granted her request. He could not change what he had already written and sealed. But he could make a new law giving the Jews permission to kill any enemies who tried to harm them. He had letters written to give the Jews this right. Mordecai told the scribes what to write. The letters were written and sealed with the king's ring so that no man could change what was written. They were written in the name of the king to all the people ruled by King Ahasuerus. They were written in different languages so that all the people could read them.

Men were sent out on horseback, mules, and camels to bring the message to all people. In the message was written that the Jews had permission from the king to kill anyone who would try to hurt them on the day that Haman had appointed that they should be killed.

Mordecai went out from the king in royal clothes of blue and white and with a great crown of gold. The city of Shushan rejoiced and was glad. Mordecai would be a good ruler.

The Jews were honored and had joy and gladness. Their sorrow was turned to joy. In every city where the people received the command of the king, the Jews feasted with joy and gladness

60

and had a good day.

Many people in the land became Jews because they were afraid. God was with the Jews. He was helping them.

At last the thirteenth day of the twelfth month came. The Jews were ready to kill anyone who might try to kill them. No one could overcome them because the people were afraid of them. The Lord was on their side. The king was on their side. All the rulers and officers of the king helped the Jews. They were afraid to do otherwise, because Mordecai the Jew was a great man and was becoming greater and greater.

The Jews killed their enemies. In Shushan the palace, five hundred men were killed. Haman's ten sons were killed. Word was brought to the king to tell him how many had been killed.

The king said to Esther, "The Jews have destroyed five hundred men at Shushan the palace and the ten sons of Haman. What have they done in the other provinces? Now what is your petition? It shall be given you. What is your request further? It shall be done."

Esther answered, "If it please the king, let the Jews do tomorrow as they have done today. Let Haman's ten sons be hanged upon the gallows."

The king commanded that this be done. So on the fourteenth day of the twelfth month many more men were killed. Thus the enemies of the Jews were destroyed. On the fifteenth day they rested and had a day of feasting and gladness.

After this Mordecai wrote letters. He sent them to all the Jews in all the provinces of the king, both near and far. In the letters he wrote that every year on the fourteenth and fifteenth days of the twelfth month they should hold a feast. They were to send good things to one another and give gifts to the poor. The feast was to be in memory of the days when God had given them victory over their enemies. It was to be celebrated in the same way as they had celebrated it that day, feasting with joy and gladness because their sorrow was turned to joy, and their mourning to a good day.

The Jews did as Mordecai had written to them. These days were to be remembered in every generation, in every family, in all the land ruled by Ahasuerus, and in every city. Many Jews still keep this feast today. It is called the feast of Purim.

Mordecai was put next in power to the king. The Jews looked up to him as a great man. He

62

was great because he feared God and was kind to all his people, the Jews. He did what was best for them and spoke words of peace to them.

Ezra Helps His People

Ezra 7

Ezra, a priest of God and a good teacher in the Law of Moses, was in Babylon. But he wanted to go to Jerusalem to teach the people there.

It was nearly eighty years since the first group had left Babylon to go to Jerusalem. They had gone with Zerubbabel the governor and Jeshua the priest to start building the temple. All these people were now probably dead. Even their children were old by this time. It was about sixty years since the temple had been finished.

God was good to Ezra. He caused King Artaxerxes to give him permission to go to Jerusalem. So Ezra diligently prepared his heart to obey God and to go and teach the people of Israel.

Before he left, King Artaxerxes gave Ezra a letter to take along. This is what the king wrote to Ezra:

Artaxerxes, king of kings,

To Ezra the priest, a scribe of the Law of the

64

God of heaven. Perfect peace, and at such a time.

I make a law that all the people of Israel who desire of their own free will to go up to Jerusalem, go with you. You have been sent by the king and his seven counselors to find out how things are going at Jerusalem according to the law of your God which is in your hand.

Carry all the silver and gold which the king and his counselors have freely offered to the God of Israel. Take all the silver and gold that you can find in the land of Babylon. Take it along with the freewill offering of the people and of the priests which they offer willingly for the house of their God which is in Jerusalem. Take it that you may quickly buy bullocks, rams, and lambs with their meat offerings and drink offerings. Offer them upon the altar of the house of your God which is in Jerusalem.

Whatever seems good to you and to your brethren to do with the rest of the silver and the gold, do according to the will of your God. Also deliver before the God of Jerusalem the vessels that have been given to you for the service of the house of your God. Whatever else you need for the house of your God, take it out of the king's treasure house.

And I, even I, Artaxerxes the king, make a law to all the treasurers which are beyond the river. Whatever Ezra the priest, the scribe of the law of the God of heaven, shall ask of you, let it be done speedily.

Whatever is commanded by the God of heaven, let it be done diligently for the house of the God of heaven.

Also, concerning the priests, Levites, singers, porters, or ministers of the house of God, it will not be lawful to make them pay taxes.

And you, Ezra, after the wisdom of your God which is in your hand, set up officers and judges who can judge all the people who are beyond the river. Use those who know God's laws to teach those who do not know God's laws.

Whoever will not obey the law of your God and the law of the king, let him be punished speedily, whether by death, by banishment, by taking away his goods, or by putting him in prison.

Ezra was deeply thankful and encouraged to receive such a letter from the king. He blessed the Lord, because He had put in the king's heart a desire to beautify the temple at Jerusalem.

Ezra was strengthened by the hand of the Lord his God upon him. He gathered together out of Israel chief men to go with him to Jerusalem.

Lesson 15

Joy and Sorrow

Ezra 8; 9

Ezra and all the people who were with him gathered together at a river. There they camped in tents for three days. Ezra looked over the people. He did not see any of the sons of Levi there. He sent for them so that there would be ministers for the house of God when the people arrived at Jerusalem. God was good to them and caused men of understanding to be brought to them.

While the people were there by the river, they fasted and prayed before God. Ezra had been ashamed to ask the king for soldiers to help them fight enemies along the way. They had told the king that their God was with them to protect them if they trusted in Him. They had also told him that God's power and anger are against those who do not obey Him. Now they fasted and prayed to God to show them a safe way to go up to Jerusalem. God heard them and answered their prayer.

Ezra separated twenty-two of the chief priests and their brethren from the others in the group. To these he weighed and gave the offering of gold and silver, and the vessels of silver, gold, and fine copper. He said to them, "You are holy unto the Lord. The vessels also are holy. The silver and the gold are a freewill offering to the Lord God of your fathers. Watch these things and keep them until you weigh them before the chief of the priests and the Levites and the chief of the fathers of Israel at Jerusalem."

After this they left the river and started on their way to Jerusalem. The Lord was with them to deliver them from their enemies who were waiting to harm them. God was against their enemies so that they had no power to hurt His people.

It was a long way from Babylon to Jerusalem. Yet it took only four months to go because God was with them.

When they arrived at Jerusalem, they waited for three days. On the fourth day, the silver and the gold and the vessels were weighed in the house of God. The number of them and the weight of them were written down. The people offered burnt offerings to the Lord. The letter from the king was

68

given to the king's officers and governors. Then they helped the people in the work in the house of the Lord as the king had commanded.

When all this was finished, the princes came to Ezra with distressing news. The Jews who were living in the land of Judah were disobeying God. They had married wives and husbands of the people of the land of Canaan who were not Jews. These people did not love the true God. They caused the people of Israel to do the evil things that they did. The princes and the rulers were the main ones in this sin.

When Ezra heard this, his joy turned to sorrow. He tore his clothes. He pulled out the hair of his head and beard. Then he sat down, not knowing what to do. God could not bless them while such evil was among them.

Everyone who was afraid to disobey the Lord gathered together with Ezra. They trembled at God's Word because of those who disobeyed. Ezra sat stunned until the evening sacrifice.

At the evening sacrifice, Ezra arose, fell on his knees, and spread out his hands to the Lord his God. He said, "O my God, I am ashamed and blush to lift up my face to You, my God. Our sins have increased over our heads, and our trespass

69

has grown up to the heavens. Since the days of our fathers we have been in great trespass until now.

"Because of our sins, we, our kings, and our priests have been delivered into the hand of the kings of the lands. And now for a little space kindness has been shown to us from the Lord our God to let a few of us escape. This was done so that our God may lighten our eyes and give us a little reviving in our slavery, for we were slaves. Yet our God has not forsaken us in our slavery but has given mercy to us in the sight of the kings of Persia. He did this to give us a reviving to set up the house of our God and to repair it, and to give us a wall in Judah and Jerusalem.

"Now, O our God, what shall we say after this? For we have forsaken Your commandments. The prophets said, 'The land which you go to possess is an unclean land. Because of this, do not give your daughters to their sons, neither take their daughters for your sons. Do not seek their peace or their wealth forever so that you may be strong and eat the good of the land and leave it for an inheritance to your children forever.'

"After all this that has come upon us because of our sin, seeing that God has punished us less

70

than we deserve, and has given us such deliverance as this, should we break Your commandments again? Should we join the people of this wickedness? Would You not be angry with us until You have destroyed us so that none are left? O Lord God of Israel, You are righteous. We still remain escaped as we are today. We are before You in our sins. We cannot stand before You because of this.''

Lesson 16

The People Repent

Ezra 10:1-19

Ezra was not alone as he prayed, confessing and crying before the house of God. Many of the people of Israel—men, women, and children—came to Ezra and cried in great distress.

One of the men said to Ezra, "We have sinned against the Lord and have taken strange wives of the people of the land. Yet now there is hope in Israel about this thing. Because of this, let us make an agreement with our God to put away all the wives and the children which were born to them. Let us do according to what you and those who tremble at the commandment of our God say. Let it be done according to the Law. Get up, because you are responsible to see that this is done. We also will be with you. Be of good courage and do it."

Ezra got up. He made the chief priests and the Levites and all Israel promise to do as this man said. They all promised to do this.

Ezra went from before the temple into the

72

room of one of the men. He would not eat bread nor drink water because of the sins of the people. Sin is a very serious matter, and Ezra was wise to take it seriously.

An announcement was made throughout all Judah and Jerusalem to all the children of the captives. It was announced that they should gather together at Jerusalem. It was also announced that they should come within three days. If they would not, their things would be taken away from them and they would be separated from the rest of the people.

Within three days all the men of Judah and Benjamin gathered together at Jerusalem. All the people sat in the street of God's house. They trembled because of the seriousness of their sin, and also because of the great rain.

Ezra the priest stood up. He said to the people, "You have sinned and have taken strange wives to increase the sin of Israel. Because of this, make a confession to the Lord God of your fathers. Do what He wants you to do. Separate yourselves from the people of the land and from the strange wives."

All the congregation answered Ezra with a loud voice. They said, "As you have said, so must we do. But there are many people, and it is a very rainy time. We are not able to stand outside. Neither is this a work that can be done in one or two days, because there are many of us who have sinned in this thing."

They suggested further, "Appoint a certain time for the people who have taken strange wives to come to the rulers and older men and judges to have this matter settled."

This they did. In about two months everything was settled. The men promised to put away their strange wives and the children born to them. They offered a sacrifice for their sin.

Lesson 17

Nehemiah's Request

Nehemiah 1:1–2:8

Nearly thirteen years after Ezra and his group had gone to Jerusalem, visitors came from the land of Judah to Persia.

Nehemiah, a Jew, was working in Shushan the palace at this time. He served the king of Persia his drinks. Therefore, he was called the king's cupbearer. Nehemiah was eager to hear how his Jewish brethren at Jerusalem were getting along. He asked these visitors from Judah about them and about Jerusalem.

They said, "Those who are left there are in great trouble and disgrace. The wall of Jerusalem is broken down, and the gates of the wall are burned with fire."

Nehemiah was very sorry to hear this. To all Jews who loved God, Jerusalem was the dearest spot on earth because it was the city of God's house. Nehemiah sat down and cried when he heard the sad news about Jerusalem. For a number of days he mourned and fasted and

75

prayed to the God of heaven. He said, "I beg of You, O Lord God of heaven, the great and terrible God, who keeps His agreement and mercy for those who love Him and keep His commandments. Let Your ears be attentive and Your eyes open that You may hear the prayer of Your servant which I pray before You day and night. I pray and confess the sins of the children of Israel which we have sinned against You. Both I and my father's house have sinned. We have sinned terribly before You and have not kept the commandments that You commanded Your servant Moses. Remember, I beg of You, what You said to Moses. You said, 'If you sin, I will scatter you among the nations. But if you turn to Me and keep My commandments and do them, I will gather you and bring you to the place that I have chosen to put My Name.' Now these are Your servants and Your people whom You have redeemed by Your great power and by Your strong hand. O Lord, I beg of You, listen to the prayer of Your servant and the prayer of Your servants who want to fear Your Name. Please help me to find mercy in the sight of this man."

When Nehemiah said, "this man," he was speaking about the king. He wanted the king to

76

show mercy to him and let him go to Jerusalem to help in the work there.

About four months later, Nehemiah took wine and gave it to the king. Before this time, Nehemiah had not been sad in the presence of the king. Now the king saw that Nehemiah looked sad.

The king said to Nehemiah, "Why do you look sad when you are not sick? This is nothing else but sorrow of heart."

Nehemiah was very much afraid. He said to the king, "Let the king live forever. Why should not my face be sad when the city where my fathers' graves are lies neglected, and the gates are burned with fire?"

The king asked Nehemiah, "For what do you make request?"

Nehemiah prayed to the God of heaven. God could help him to give the right answer to the king. He said, "If it please the king, and if your servant has found favor in your sight, send me to Judah, to the city of my fathers' graves, that I may build it."

The king, with the queen sitting by him, asked Nehemiah, "For how long shall your journey be? When will you return?"

Nehemiah told the king how long he wished to be gone. He also said, "If it please the king, let letters be given to me for the governors who are on the other side of the river so that they carry me over until I come to Judah. Give me also a letter for the keeper of the king's forest so that he will give me timber to make beams for the gates of the palace and for the walls of the city and for the house into which I shall come."

The king granted Nehemiah his request. It was according to the good hand of Nehemiah's God upon him that the king showed this favor.

Lesson 18

Nehemiah Goes to Jerusalem
Nehemiah 2:9–3:32

Nehemiah started for Jerusalem, attended by captains of the army and horsemen whom the king sent with him. When they came to the governors on the other side of the river, they gave them the letters from the king. At last Nehemiah and his men arrived at Jerusalem.

After Nehemiah had been at Jerusalem for three days, he and a few men got up during the night. Nehemiah wanted to see the condition of Jerusalem for himself. He had no animal with him except the one on which he rode. He had not told anyone what his God had put in his heart to do at Jerusalem. He went out by the gate of the valley and looked over the walls of Jerusalem. They were broken down, and the gates were burned with fire. Nehemiah went on to the gate of the fountain and to the king's pool. But there was no place for the animal on which he was riding to pass.

Then Nehemiah went up by the brook to look

79

at more of the wall. He came back again through the gate of the valley and returned to his place.

The rulers did not know where Nehemiah went or what he did. He had not yet told the Jews, the priests, the rulers, or the workers why he had come.

After he had seen for himself the condition of the walls, he was ready to tell the people there why he had come. He said, "You see the distress that we are in, how Jerusalem is in ruins and the gates are burned with fire. Come and let us build up the wall of Jerusalem so that we will not be a disgrace any longer." Nehemiah told them that the hand of his God had been good upon him and that the king had sent him and had helped him to come.

The men were encouraged when they heard this. They said, "Let us get up and build." They made their hands strong for this good work.

Now two men, Sanballat and Tobiah, heard that Nehemiah had come to help the people at Jerusalem. They did not like this at all, for they were enemies of the Jews. It grieved them exceedingly. They, and Geshem with them, laughed at the Jews and made fun of them. They despised them and said to them, "What is this that you are doing? Will you rebel against the king?"

Nehemiah answered them, "The God of heaven will prosper us. Therefore we, His servants, will get up and build. But you have no part or right in Jerusalem."

The work was well organized. Each man had his own job to do to help out in the great work. There were men repairing the wall all the way around Jerusalem. Each group of men had its own special part to repair.

Lesson 19

Enemies Try to Hinder the Work
Nehemiah 4

When Sanballat heard that the Jews were actually building the wall, he was angry. He joked about them to his own people and to the army around him. He said, "What are these feeble Jews doing? Will they make themselves strong? Will they sacrifice? Will they finish in one day? Will they make good use again of the stones out of the heaps of the rubbish which are burned?"

Tobiah was with Sanballat. He also made fun of the Jews and their work. He said, "If even a fox went on what they build, it would break down their stone wall."

Yes, they were making fun of the Jews before their own people. They were calling them feeble. They were saying that their wall was so weak that a fox could break it down.

But Nehemiah knew what to do when they laughed at him and despised him. He prayed to his God and kept on working. The work was going well and fast because the people had a mind to

82

work.

Finally Sanballat and Tobiah and the other people around them heard that the walls were up. They heard that the cracks and holes in the walls were beginning to be repaired. Now they were very angry. They decided to go up and fight against the city and hinder the work.

Again the Jews knew what to do. They prayed to their God and set men to watch for the enemy day and night.

Now round about Jerusalem were great heaps of rubbish. These big heaps hindered the men who were trying to build the wall. There were burden bearers whose job was to haul the rubbish away. But this was hard work, and their strength was giving out. They could not get the rubbish out of the way very fast. Some of the people reported, "The strength of the burden bearers is weakening, and there is much rubbish, so that we are not able to build the wall."

But the Jews' enemies liked the rubbish. They saw the big heaps as being good places for them to sneak in and hide. Then when they had a chance, they would come out of their hiding places and kill the Jews.

But the Jews who lived among these enemies

heard of the enemies' plans. They came to Jerusalem and warned the people what their enemies were planning to do.

So Nehemiah put men with their families in both the high and the low places round about. He gave them swords and spears and bows. He encouraged them, "Do not be afraid. Remember your great God and fight to save your brethren, your families, and your houses."

Their enemies heard that Israel had found out their plans. They knew that they could not sneak in and kill them now. Then the people went back to work on the wall. But they still were on the watch. From that time on, half the servants worked on the wall. The other half watched for an attack from their enemies. They held spears, shields, and other weapons in their hands.

Those who built the wall, those who carried away rubbish, and all the other workers, worked with one hand and held a weapon in the other. The man to sound the trumpet was with Nehemiah. If he knew that the enemies were coming, he would blow the trumpet to warn the people.

Nehemiah said to the rulers and to all the people, "The work is great and large. We are separated on the wall, one far from another.

84

Wherever you are, when you hear the sound of the trumpet, come to us. Our God shall fight for us."

The people labored together in the work. Half of them held the spears from early morning until the stars appeared at night. During the night they slept inside Jerusalem with their clothes on. That way they could be ready to get up and fight enemies at any time, if it were necessary. The people changed their clothes only when they needed to be washed. While the people slept, watchmen watched for the enemies and guarded the people.

Lesson 20

Trouble in Judah

Nehemiah 5

After Nehemiah was governor in Judah for a while, he heard something that made him very sad. This time it was not Sanballat, Tobiah, or any other enemies causing them trouble. The Jews were having trouble among themselves. There was a great famine, and the rich Jews were not treating their poorer brethren fairly.

Because of this, the poor were becoming poorer and poorer. Some of these poor people had to sell their lands and houses in order to have enough to eat. Some of them had to mortgage their lands or borrow money in order to have money to buy food and pay their taxes. Already some of their daughters had to go for slaves. Even some of their sons were in danger of becoming slaves to the rich. The rich who loaned money were charging the poor more interest on the borrowed money than what they were able to pay. Things were becoming so bad that the poor were crying out against their richer brethren.

When Nehemiah heard the cry of the poor, he was very angry. It was not right that the rich Jews should treat their poor brethren so unfairly and cruelly. God had commanded His people to be kind and fair to the poor and to help them.

Nehemiah thought over the whole matter. Then he scolded the rulers. He said, "You have charged your poor brethren interest on the money they borrowed to pay their taxes. He told the rulers, "We, as much as we could, have helped our brethren, the Jews, who were sold to the heathen. Will you even sell your brethren, or shall they be sold to us?"

The nobles and the rulers did not answer Nehemiah. They could think of nothing to say. They knew that they were guilty of a great wrong.

God had told them in His Law to Moses how to treat their brethren. They were not to charge extra money when they loaned money to their brethren.

Nehemiah reminded the rich Jews that they were not giving a good testimony to their enemies. Their enemies would see that they were not treating one another fairly. He told them to quit charging their brethren interest on the money they loaned. He said, "Please give back to them

87

their lands, vineyards, olive yards, and houses to-day. Also give back to them the interest that you asked of them."

They replied, "We will give these things back to them. We will not ask them to give us anything. We will do as you have told us."

Nehemiah called for the priests. He asked them to promise to do this also. They made the promise.

Then Nehemiah shook out his lap. He said, "So let God shake out every man from his house and from his work if he does not keep this promise. Even this way let him be shaken out and emptied."

All the congregation said, "Amen," and praised the Lord. The people did as they had promised.

Nehemiah had set a good example for the people. He did not ask them to do anything that he himself had not done or was not willing to do. Though he was the governor over the people, he had not been unfair to them. He did not expect them to feed him, as the governors before him had done. He was willing to work. He worked with the people in the building of the wall. He knew that the people had a hard time making a living.

Nehemiah asked God to remember him for the good he had done to these people.

Lesson 21

The Enemy Tries Again

Nehemiah 6:1-14

At last the wall around Jerusalem was built, and all the broken places in the wall were repaired. Sanballat, Tobiah, Geshem, and the other enemies of the Jews heard this. So far their plans to hinder and to destroy the work had failed. They had mocked and made fun of the workmen. They had tried to kill them and could not. Still they would not give up. They had a different plan. They decided to act friendly to the Jews. Perhaps in this way, they could deceive the people. The gates of the city were not yet set up, and the enemies did not want them to be set up.

Sanballat and Geshem sent a message to Nehemiah. They said, "Come, let us meet together in a village in the plain of Ono."

Nehemiah was not easily fooled. He knew they were trying to do mischief. He sent messengers to them with this message from him: "I am doing a great work, so that I cannot come down. Why should the work stop while I leave it and come

90

down to you?"

The enemies still would not give up. Again and again they invited Nehemiah to come and meet with them. Four more times they sent their request.

Each time Nehemiah sent the same kind of answer back to them. He would not be persuaded. He would stand firm, busy in the work of the Lord.

The fifth time Sanballat sent his servant to Nehemiah with an open letter. He was trying a new scheme. In the letter he said:

> It is reported among the heathen, and Gashmu says it, that you and the Jews are planning to rebel. The reason you are building the wall is that you want to be king. You have also appointed prophets to preach about you at Jerusalem and to say, "There is a king in Judah." Now what you have said shall be reported to the king. Because of this, come and let us talk about it together.

Of course, if this were true, and if the king heard about it, their lives would be in danger. But it was not true. Nehemiah sent this word back to Sanballat:

> There are no such things done as you say.

You are just making it up out of your own heart.

Nehemiah knew that his enemies were trying to hinder him and his people in the work. Sanballat was trying to make them afraid. He was trying to weaken their hands so that the work would not get done. Nehemiah prayed to God for strength.

Tobiah and Sanballat were truly having a hard time with Nehemiah. Their schemes were not working. Nehemiah had a wise and strong God in whom he trusted. Nehemiah would not let anyone make him afraid and stop working.

But God's enemies do not give up easily. They had still another scheme to try. They would try to get Nehemiah to sin. If he sinned, the Lord would not be with him to strengthen him. The enemies then hired a man to pretend that he was a prophet of God. This man came to Nehemiah and said, "Let us meet together in the house of God inside the temple. Let us shut the doors of the temple because they will come to kill you. Yes, in the night they will come to kill you."

Nehemiah knew that they were trying to make him afraid. He knew that God had not sent this man. It would be sin to listen to him and be afraid and go into the temple. If Nehemiah sinned, his

92

enemies could truly speak evil of him. Nehemiah said to the false prophet, "Should a man like me run for my life? I will not go in."

Again Nehemiah prayed to his God. He said, "My God, think about Tobiah and Sanballat according to these words of theirs. Think about the prophetess Noadiah and the other prophets who want to make me afraid." Nehemiah could trust his God to deal with each of the enemies in the best way.

Lesson 22

Ezra Teaches the People

Nehemiah 6:15–8:6

In fifty-two days the wall of Jerusalem was finished. The Jews' enemies and all the heathen heard that the wall was finished. They felt discouraged. All their efforts to hinder the work had failed. They knew that the work was done because of the God of Israel.

Tobiah had married one of the Israelites' daughters. Because of this, he had many dealings with the nobles in Israel. He sent many letters to them, and they sent many letters to him. The nobles seemed to think that Tobiah was a good man. They told Nehemiah what good deeds he had done. Then they told Tobiah what Nehemiah said. Tobiah sent letters to Nehemiah to make him afraid.

But Nehemiah went right on working. The wall was finished and the doors were set up. Still there was work to be done. Jerusalem was a great and large city. But there were not many people in it. The men had been busy working on the wall.

94

They had not yet built houses for themselves in Jerusalem. These people needed rulers to rule over them. They needed watchmen to protect them.

Nehemiah appointed two men to be rulers in Jerusalem. The one ruler was his brother. The other man was the ruler of the palace. He was a faithful man. He feared God more than many of the other men. Nehemiah told these two men, "Do not let the gates of Jerusalem be opened until the sun is hot. Appoint watchmen to carefully guard the people in the city."

God put into the heart of Nehemiah a desire to gather the people together to find the record of the families to which they belonged. There were a few who could not tell from which family they had come. They could not prove that they were Jews. None of these men were allowed to be priests. They were considered to be unclean.

Altogether there were 42,360 people in the whole congregation of Israel. Besides them, there were 7,337 menservants and maidservants, and 245 singing men and women. They had 736 horses, 245 mules, 735 camels, and 6,720 donkeys.

All the people gathered together as one man in the street in front of the water gate. They asked Ezra the scribe to bring the Book of the Law of

Moses.

On the first day of the seventh month, Ezra the priest brought the Law before the congregation of men and women. He stood on a pulpit of wood which had been made especially for him. By standing on the wooden pulpit, he was above the people, and they could see him better. Six men stood on the right side of Ezra, and seven men stood on his left side. Ezra opened the Book of the Law in the sight of all the people. When Ezra opened the Book, all the people stood up. Ezra blessed the Lord, the great God.

All the people answered, "Amen, Amen," as they lifted up their hands. They bowed their heads and worshiped the Lord with their faces toward the ground.

From morning until noon Ezra read to the people. Everyone listened carefully to what was being read. God was speaking to them.

Lesson 23

The People Obey the Law
Nehemiah 8:7–9:8

Thirteen men besides the Levites helped the people to understand the Law. They read in the Book of the Law distinctly. They told the people what the words meant and helped them to understand the reading.

The people wept when they heard the reading. Their teachers said to them, "Today is holy to the Lord your God. Do not mourn or weep. Go your way. Eat and drink and send gifts to those who have nothing prepared, because this day is holy unto our Lord. Do not be sorry, for the joy of the Lord is your strength." By these words, the Levites were able to comfort the people and quiet them.

All the people went their way. They ate and drank. They sent gifts and had a good time because they understood what had been read to them.

On the second day, the chief fathers of all the people and the priests and Levites gathered

98

together with Ezra. They wanted to understand what was written in the Law. They found that the Lord had commanded by Moses that the children of Israel should live in booths during the Feast of Tabernacles. This feast came every year in the seventh month. It was at the time of the year that the people finished harvesting their crops. The feast lasted seven days. It was a joyous time. The eighth day was also kept holy. The people were not to do any extra work on that day.

The leaders said to the people, "Go to the mountain. Gather branches to make booths to live in. Gather olive branches, pine branches, myrtle branches, palm branches, and branches of thick trees."

The people did this. They went to the mountain and gathered branches. From the branches they made booths and sat under these shelters. The children of Israel had not done this since the days of Joshua. There was great gladness among them, for gladness comes from obeying the Lord.

Each day of the feast, from the first day to the last, Ezra read in the Book of the Law of God. The people kept the feast seven days and had a solemn meeting on the eighth day.

On the ninth day the children of Israel again

gathered together. This time they fasted, putting sackcloth and earth on themselves. They separated themselves from strangers and confessed their sins and the sins of their fathers. They spent one-half of the ninth day together. Half of this time the Book of the Law was read to them. The other half of the time the people confessed and worshiped the Lord.

Then some of the Levites stood up on the stairs. They cried with a loud voice to the Lord their God. They said, "Stand up and bless the Lord your God for ever and ever. Blessed be Your glorious Name, which is higher than all blessing and praise. You, even You, are Lord alone. You have made heaven, the heaven of heavens, with all their host; the earth, and all things that are in it; the seas, and all that is in them. You keep them all, and the host of heaven worships You.

"You are the Lord, the God who chose Abram and brought him out of Ur of the Chaldees. You gave him the name Abraham. You found his heart faithful to You. You made a promise with him to give this land to his children. You have done as You said You would, because You are righteous."

Lesson 24

The Prayer Continued

Nehemiah 9:9-31

The Levites continued their prayer to God. They said, "You saw the affliction of our fathers in Egypt. You heard their cry by the Red Sea. You showed signs and wonders on Pharaoh and on all his servants and on all the people of his land. You knew that they acted proudly against Your people. So You got Yourself a Name as it is today. You divided the sea in front of Your people so that they went through the middle of the sea on dry ground. You threw those who tried to hurt them into the depths, as a stone into mighty waters.

"Besides this, You led them during the day by a cloudy pillar. And in the night You led them by a pillar of fire to give them light in the way that they should go.

"You came down also on Mount Sinai. You spoke with them from heaven. You gave them right judgments, true laws, and good commandments. You made known to them Your holy Sabbath and commanded them laws by the hand

101

of Moses, Your servant.

"You gave them bread from heaven for their hunger. You brought water out of the rock for their thirst. You promised them that they should go in to possess the land that You had agreed to give them.

"But they and our fathers acted proudly and were stubborn. They did not listen to Your commandments. They refused to obey. Neither did they think about Your wonders that You did among them. They were stubborn. And in their rebellion they appointed a captain to take them back to the place where they had been in slavery.

"But You are a God ready to pardon, gracious, and merciful, slow to anger, and of great kindness. You did not forsake them. They made a molten calf and called it the god that brought them up out of Egypt. They did great things to make You angry. Yet You in Your many mercies did not forsake them in the wilderness. The pillar of cloud did not depart from them by day to lead them in the way. Neither did the pillar of fire depart by night to show them light and the way in which they should go.

"You gave also Your good Spirit to teach them. You did not keep back manna from their mouths. You gave them water for their thirst. Yes, forty years You kept them supplied in the wilderness so that they lacked nothing. Their clothes did not become old, and their feet did not swell.

"Besides this, You gave them kingdoms and nations and divided them into portions. You also multiplied their children as the stars of heaven. You brought them into the land that You promised to their fathers. So their children went in and possessed the land. You overcame the Canaanites with their kings and the people of the land before them so that they might do with them as they wished. They took strong cities and a good land. They owned houses full of all goods. They digged wells and had vineyards, olive yards, and fruit trees in abundance. They ate and were filled. They became rich and delighted themselves in Your great goodness.

"Yet with all this, they were disobedient and rebelled against You. They threw the Law behind their backs. They killed Your prophets who told them of their evil so that they would turn back to You. They did many things to provoke You.

"Because of this, You delivered them into the hand of their enemies, who troubled them. When they cried to You in the time of their trouble, You heard them from heaven. According to Your many mercies, You gave them saviors who saved them out of the hand of their enemies. After they had rest, they again did evil before You. For that reason, You left them in the hand of their enemies so that their enemies ruled over them. Yet when they returned and cried to You, You heard them from heaven. Many times You delivered them according to Your mercies.

"You testified against them that You might bring them again to Your Law. Yet they acted proudly and would not listen to Your commandments, but sinned against Your judgments. They were stubborn and would not listen to Your commandments.

"Yet for many years You were patient with them and testified against them by Your Spirit in Your prophets. Yet they would not listen. Therefore You gave them into the hand of the people of the lands. In spite of this, because of Your great mercy, You did not altogether destroy them nor forsake them; for You are a gracious and merciful God."

Lesson 25

The People's Promises

Nehemiah 9:32–13:3

The Levites still continued their prayer to God. They knew God was great and mighty. They knew He keeps His promises and shows mercy. They prayed, "Do not let all the trouble that has come on us seem little to You. Yet You are just in all that has been brought upon us. You have done right, but we have done wickedly. Neither have our kings, our princes, our priests, nor our fathers kept the Law. Nor have they listened to Your commandments and Your testimonies, which You testified against them. They have not served You in their kingdom and in Your great goodness that You gave them and in the large and good land that You gave before them. Neither did they turn from their wicked works.

"See, we are servants now in the land that You gave to our fathers. You gave it to them so that we could eat the fruit of it and the good of it. It gives much increase to the kings that You have set over us because of our sins. Also they rule over

105

our bodies and over our cattle however it pleases them, and we are in great distress. Because of all this, we make a sure promise and write it. Our princes, Levites, and priests seal it."

Thus their prayer was ended and their sure promise was written. This writing was signed by Nehemiah and by many other leaders of the Jews. All the other Jews who had separated themselves from the people of the land to keep God's Law agreed to what had been written and signed. They said, "We will keep all the commandments of God. We will not let our sons or our daughters marry the people of the land. If the people of the land bring anything to us to sell on the Sabbath Day, we will not buy it from them on the Sabbath Day or on a holy day."

In the Law of Moses it was written that every seventh year the people should not plant crops. If any plants came up of themselves that year, they were not to harvest the fruit they bore. Also, in the seventh year if any poor person owed them a debt, they were to forgive that debt. They were not to make the person pay the debt. The people promised to do these things.

Rules were also made about bringing offerings to the Lord. Usually when the first fruits or

106

vegetables get ripe, we are eager to eat them. But the people promised to bring the first ripe fruit to the Lord. They also promised to bring the first-born of their sons and of their herds and of their flocks to the house of the Lord. Besides these offerings, they promised to give to the Lord one-tenth of all that they received.

There was a dedication for the wall at Jerusalem. On that day the people brought great thanksgiving to God. They offered great sacrifices and rejoiced with the great joy God had given them. The wives and the children rejoiced so that the joy of Jerusalem was heard a long way off. On that day the leaders read in the Book of Moses before all the people. There they found written that the Ammonite and the Moabite should not come into the congregation of God forever. This was because they had not been kind to the children of Israel in giving them food and water. Instead, they had hired Balaam to curse them. Yet, in spite of this, God had turned the curse into a blessing for Israel.

When the people heard what was written in the Law, they obeyed it. They separated themselves from the people who were not true Israelites.

Lesson 26

More Work to Do

Nehemiah 13:4-31

After Nehemiah had been at Jerusalem for a while, he went back to the king at Babylon. The king, however, gave him permission to come back to Jerusalem again. In the time that Nehemiah was gone from Jerusalem, one of the high priests had joined himself to Tobiah. He had even prepared a great room for him in the house of the Lord.

When Nehemiah returned, he learned what a wicked thing this priest had done. He was very much grieved. He threw all Tobiah's things out of the room. He commanded the room to be thoroughly cleaned. Then he brought in the vessels for the house of God.

Nehemiah saw that the Levites were not doing their work in the house of the Lord. They had gone out to their fields. Then he found out why they had left Jerusalem to work in their fields. They were not getting what belonged to them. The Levites were to do the work of the house of the

108

Lord. The people had promised to give the Lord one-tenth of all they received. They were to give this tithe to the Levites so that they would have enough to eat without going out and working in their fields. Nehemiah asked the rulers, "Why is the house of God forsaken?"

4 Nehemiah gathered the Levites together. He set them in their place in the house of God. He had the people bring in their tithes so that the Levites had enough to eat without working in their fields. If they spent all their time in the fields, then the house of God would be neglected.

5 In those days Nehemiah saw in Judah some who were working on the Sabbath Day. They loaded up the things which they had raised and brought them to Jerusalem on the Sabbath Day. Nehemiah told them, "It is wrong for you to do this."

6 Other men brought fish and other kinds of things to Jerusalem. They sold them to the Jews on the Sabbath Day. Nehemiah scolded the nobles of Judah for this. He said, "What evil thing is this that you do and treat the Sabbath in an unholy way? Did not your fathers do this way, and did not our God bring all this evil upon us and upon this city? Yet you bring more anger on Israel by

109

not keeping the Sabbath Day holy."

The Jews' Sabbath began on the sixth day at evening and lasted until the evening of the seventh day. Nehemiah commanded that the gates of Jerusalem be shut when the sixth day began to darken. He commanded that they should not be opened again until after the Sabbath Day ended on the next day. He set some of his servants at the gates so that no burden would be brought in on the Sabbath Day.

The people who had things to sell camped outside the wall once or twice. Nehemiah said to them, "Why do you stay by the wall? If you do this again, I will arrest you." From that time on they did not come on the Sabbath Day.

Nehemiah commanded the Levites to purify themselves. He told them to come and watch the gates so that the Sabbath Day might be kept holy.

In those days Nehemiah saw some Jews who had married women of Moab and Ammon. Their children could not speak the Hebrew language. Nehemiah scolded them and cursed them. He hit some of them and pulled out their hair. He made them promise not to let their sons or their daughters marry the Moabites or Ammonites. He

110

said, "Did not Solomon, king of Israel, sin by these things? Among many nations there was no king like him, who was beloved of his God. God made him king over all Israel. Yet outlandish women caused even him to sin. Shall we then listen to you to let you do this great evil to disobey God in marrying strange wives?"

(0 The grandson of the high priest had married the daughter of Sanballat. Because of this, Nehemiah chased him away. Nehemiah was very diligent to correct things that were not right and to do according to the Law of his God. He prayed, "Remember me, O my God, for good."

Lesson 27

The Story of Jonah
Part 1
Jonah 1:1-16

Jonah was a prophet of God. He lived about the same time as the prophet Elisha.

The Lord said to Jonah, "Arise, and go to Nineveh, that great city. Preach against it because the wickedness of the people of Nineveh is come up before Me."

The people of Nineveh were heathen people. Jonah did not want to go there. Who would want to go up and down the streets of their city and tell the people that they were wicked? Who would want to tell them that their city would be destroyed? To preach this would not be pleasant or easy. The people might think that Jonah was crazy. They might shut him up in prison to keep him from disturbing them.

Yet, Jonah was not so much afraid of what they would do to him as he was of something else. He believed that the people of Nineveh might

112

repent of their sins. Then, if they were sorry for their sins and obeyed God, God would not destroy them. God would spare them and their city. Jonah did not want to preach that they would be destroyed if God would not destroy them after all.

We do not know what all went through Jonah's mind. We do know that he was not ready to obey God. He wanted to get away from God.

Instead of going east to the great city of Nineveh, Jonah went in the opposite direction. He went down to Joppa, a city along the seacoast of the land of Israel.

There at Joppa, Jonah found a ship preparing to go to Tarshish, a city far away from Nineveh. Jonah paid the fare that was needed to take the trip to Tarshish. He got on the ship and went down into the ship. He was trying to get away from the Lord. But that would be impossible, for God is everywhere.

The Lord knew where Jonah was going. He saw Jonah go down into the ship. The Lord sent a great wind into the sea. It caused a mighty storm upon the waters. The wind and tempestuous waves beat so hard against the ship that it was in danger of being broken to pieces.

The sailors were afraid. Each one called upon

his god for help. They threw out the cargo of the ship in order to lighten the load on the ship. Still the storm raged.

Where was Jonah all this time? Was he afraid, too? No, Jonah did not know what danger he was in. He was lying down in the sides of the ship, fast asleep.

The master of the ship came down to Jonah. He said, "What do you mean, O sleeper? Get up and call on your God. It may be that God will think about us so that we do not die."

The men on the ship suspected that this storm was upon them because of someone's sin. They decided to cast lots to find out whose fault it was that this evil had come upon them. When they cast lots, the lot fell on Jonah, the sleeper.

The men said to Jonah, "Please tell us who is causing this evil to come upon us. What is your occupation? From where did you come? What is your country, and of what people are you?"

Jonah answered, "I am a Hebrew. I fear the Lord, the God of heaven, who made the sea and the dry land." He then told them that he had tried to run away from God.

"Why have you done this?" they asked. "What shall we do to you so that the sea will be

114

calm?'' The sea was still tempestuous, and their lives were in danger.

Jonah answered, "Take me up and throw me overboard. Then the sea will be calm for you, because I know that it is my fault that this great tempest is upon you."

But the men did not want to throw Jonah into the raging sea. They rowed hard to try to bring the ship to land. But it was impossible. The sea was churning great waves, and the wind was against them.

No, the men did not want to throw Jonah out of the ship. But they were afraid not to throw him out, too. They cried to the Lord and said, "We beg of You, O Lord, we beg of You, do not let us die for this man's life. Do not hold us guilty of killing an innocent man; for You, O Lord, have done as it pleased You."

The men then took Jonah up and threw him overboard. The sea stopped its raging and became calm. Then the men in the ship feared the Lord exceedingly. Truly Jonah's God was a great God. He could do great things. The men on the ship offered a sacrifice to the Lord and made promises to Him.

Lesson 28

The Story of Jonah

Part 2

Jonah 1:17–4:11

The Lord was not finished with Jonah. He did not let Jonah drown in the deep water. God still wanted him to go and preach to the people of Nineveh. God had prepared a great fish to swallow Jonah. So when he was cast out of the ship into the sea, a big fish opened up its mouth, and in went Jonah. The big fish swallowed, and down went Jonah into the belly of the fish.

For three days and three nights Jonah was down in the belly of the great fish. It was not comfortable there. The Lord did not want Jonah to be comfortable. He wanted Jonah to be willing to obey Him. Down in the belly of the fish it was dark and stuffy. The weeds that were in its belly wrapped around Jonah's head. Jonah was tangled with the things that the fish had eaten.

Jonah cried to the Lord in his trouble. He told the Lord that he would keep his promises and be

116

thankful.

After three days and three nights, the Lord spoke to the fish. Then the fish vomited. Out came Jonah—out of the fish's belly onto the dry ground.

The word of the Lord came to Jonah the second time. The Lord said, "Arise, go to Nineveh, that great city. Preach to it the word that I give you."

This time Jonah was willing to go. He had learned that it does not pay to try to run away from God. He arose and went to Nineveh as the Lord directed.

Nineveh was a very large city. It took three days to walk through it. As Jonah began to enter the city a day's journey, he cried, "Yet forty days and Nineveh shall be overthrown!"

The people of Nineveh believed God's message to them. Word came to the king of Nineveh about God's message through the prophet Jonah. The king got down from off his throne. He laid aside his kingly robes and covered himself with sackcloth. He sat down in ashes. He made a law and had it published all over Nineveh. The law was that neither man nor animal should eat anything, nor even drink any water. He commanded, "Let man and beast be covered with sackcloth. Cry mightily to God, and turn from your evil ways. Who can tell whether God will turn away His fierce anger so that we do not die?"

God was pleased to see the people of Nineveh take His message seriously. He was pleased to see them turn from their evil ways. Because of this, He would not have to destroy them.

But Jonah was very much displeased that God did not destroy Nineveh. He was very angry. He prayed to the Lord and said, "Please, Lord, was this not what I said when I was still in my country? That is why I ran away to Tarshish, because I knew that You are a gracious God, merciful, slow to anger, and of great kindness. Now, O Lord, I beg of You to take away my life from me because it is better for me to die than to live."

The Lord asked Jonah, "Is it right for you to be angry?"

Jonah went out of the city. He sat down on the east side of it. There he made himself a booth and sat in the shade under the booth. He wanted to see what would become of the city.

God prepared a gourd to come up over Jonah to make a shadow over his head to deliver him from his grief. Jonah was very glad for the gourd.

118

The next morning God prepared a worm which made the gourd wither. When the sun arose, God prepared a hot east wind, and the sun beat down upon Jonah.

Jonah fainted. He wished that he could die. He said, "It is better for me to die than to live."

God said to Jonah, "Is it right for you to be angry for the gourd?"

Jonah said, "I do well to be angry, even unto death."

The Lord said, "You had pity on the gourd for which you did not work and which you did not cause to grow and which came up in a night and died in a night. Should I not spare Nineveh, that great city, in which are more than 120,000 people who cannot tell the difference between their right hand and their left hand, and also much cattle?"

Lesson 29

The Books of the Old Testament

The stories in your readers for grades one, two, and three have included most of the stories in the Old Testament. There are some books in the Old Testament that we do not think of as being stories. We love these books very much, too.

The Book of Job tells the story of a godly man who suffered, and the things he learned about God.

The Book of Psalms was written mostly by King David, the shepherd boy. One of the favorite psalms is the Twenty-third Psalm. It begins, "The Lord is my shepherd; I shall not want." Psalms are songs, and we like good songs. Altogether there are one hundred fifty psalms in the Book of Psalms. It is one of the best-loved books of the Bible.

The Books of Proverbs, Ecclesiastes, and Song of Solomon were written by David's son Solomon. These books contain many wise and interesting sayings about many different things.

The last seventeen books of the Old Testa-

120

ment were written by prophets who lived during and after the times of the kings of Israel and Judah. In these books the prophets told their people what was going to happen. You have read stories about the prophets Isaiah, Jeremiah, Ezekiel, Daniel, and Jonah. There are books in the Bible that are called by their names. Jeremiah also wrote the Book of Lamentations, which comes just after the Book of Jeremiah. In this book we read of the things which Jeremiah wept about.

Besides these five prophets, there are eleven other prophets for whom books in the Old Testament are named.

The prophet Hosea lived about the same time as the prophet Isaiah. He pleaded with the people to return to the Lord. His book tells that Jesus would be called out of Egypt. We read about the fulfillment of that prophecy in Matthew, the first book of the New Testament.

The prophet Joel tells us about two kinds of worms, the cankerworm and the palmerworm. He tells about the time that the Lord would send the Holy Spirit to His people. We read about this fulfillment in the New Testament, in the second chapter of the Book of Acts.

The prophet Amos lived about the same time

as Isaiah and Hosea. He was a herdsman and also a gatherer of sycamore fruit. While he was with the flock, the Lord called him to be a prophet and to speak to the house of Israel.

Obadiah wrote a very short book. It has only one chapter. But it is a very important little book with a warning to Edom, the descendants of Esau.

Micah was a prophet who also lived about the same time as the prophets Isaiah, Hosea, and Amos. He told the people that Jesus would be born in Bethlehem.

Nahum, like Joel, talks about the cankerworm. He gives warning to the great city of Nineveh. Although the people of Nineveh had repented at the preaching of Jonah about fifty years earlier, they had fallen back into sin. This great city was destroyed about twenty years after Nahum wrote his warning to them.

Habakkuk was told to write plainly. One of the verses in his book is a song we sing today: "The Lord is in his holy temple: let all the earth keep silence before him."

The prophet Zephaniah lived after the prophet Isaiah. In his book we often find the words "I will." Zephaniah clearly tells the people what the Lord will do.

Do you remember when the prophet Haggai lived? You read about him in one of your stories in this unit. In his book, Haggai says to the people twice, "Consider your ways." The ways of the people were not good. The Lord wanted them to take time to think what the end of their evil ways would be.

The prophet Zechariah lived about the same time as Haggai. You also read about him in one of your stories in this unit. He saw many different things and wrote about them. He told about the time that Jesus would ride on a colt into Jerusalem.

The last book of the Old Testament was written by the prophet Malachi. He is the last of the prophets that we read about until John the Baptist, who was born about four hundred years later, just before Jesus was born. Malachi tells about the coming of John the Baptist.

Lesson 30

Beautiful Writings
From the Old Testament

The writings in this lesson that are inside quotation marks (" ") are written just as they are in the Bible. These are only a very few of the many beautiful writings in the Old Testament Scriptures.

Moses wrote these words in the Book of Numbers:

"The Lord bless thee, and keep thee: the Lord make his face shine upon thee, and be gracious unto thee: the Lord lift up his countenance upon thee, and give thee peace" (Numbers 6:24-26).

Job wrote these words in the Book of Job:

"For I know that my redeemer liveth, and that he shall stand at the latter day upon the earth" (Job 19:25).

"But he knoweth the way that I take: when he hath tried me, I shall come forth as gold" (Job 23:10).

David wrote these words in the Book of

Psalms:

"I will both lay me down in peace, and sleep: for thou, Lord, only makest me dwell in safety" (Psalm 4:8).

"O Lord our Lord, how excellent is thy name in all the earth!" (Psalm 8:9).

"Thou wilt shew me the path of life: in thy presence is fulness of joy; at thy right hand there are pleasures for evermore" (Psalm 16:11).

"O taste and see that the Lord is good: blessed is the man that trusteth in him" (Psalm 34:8).

We think that David also wrote these words:

"Thy word have I hid in mine heart, that I might not sin against thee" (Psalm 119:11).

These are some words of the wise man Solomon from each of the three books that he wrote:

"Now therefore hearken unto me, O ye children: for blessed are they that keep my ways" (Proverbs 8:32).

"Even a child is known by his doings, whether his work be pure, and whether it be right" (Proverbs 20:11).

"Remember now thy Creator in the days of thy youth, while the evil days come not, nor the years draw nigh, when thou shalt say, I have no pleasure in them" (Ecclesiastes 12:1).

"The flowers appear on the earth; the time of the singing of birds is come, and the voice of the turtle is heard in our land" (Song of Solomon 2:12).

These are some beautiful verses from some of the Old Testament prophets. Those with this mark (*) are about Jesus.

*"When Israel was a child, then I loved him, and called my son out of Egypt" (Hosea 11:1).

"And ye shall eat in plenty, and be satisfied, and praise the name of the Lord your God, that hath dealt wondrously with you: and my people shall never be ashamed" (Joel 2:26).

"But let judgment run down as waters, and righteousness as a mighty stream" (Amos 5:24).

*"But thou, Beth-lehem Ephratah, though thou be little among the thousands of Judah, yet out of thee shall he come forth unto me that is to be ruler in Israel; whose goings forth have been from of old, from everlasting" (Micah 5:2).

"The Lord is good, a strong hold in the day of trouble; and he knoweth them that trust in him" (Nahum 1:7).

"Although the fig tree shall not blossom, neither shall fruit be in the vines; the labour of the olive shall fail, and the fields shall yield no meat; the flock shall be cut off from the fold, and there shall be no herd in the stalls: yet I will

126

rejoice in the Lord, I will joy in the God of my salvation" (Habakkuk 3:17, 18).

"The Lord thy God in the midst of thee is mighty; he will save, he will rejoice over thee with joy; he will rest in his love, he will joy over thee with singing" (Zephaniah 3:17).

"Then they that feared the Lord spake often one to another: and the Lord hearkened, and heard it, and a book of remembrance was written before him for them that feared the Lord, and that thought upon his name. And they shall be mine, saith the Lord of hosts, in that day when I make up my jewels; and I will spare them, as a man spareth his own son that serveth him" (Malachi 3:16, 17).

Unit 5

Stories About Jesus
From the Gospel of Luke

Lesson 1

The Birth of John Is Announced

Luke 1:1-23

Many people were living in the days when Jesus was born and walked here on the earth. They saw for themselves the things that Jesus did. They heard the things that He said. Others also told them things about Jesus which they had not heard or seen themselves. One of the people that told others about Jesus was Luke. He wrote a book about Jesus so that others might know that the things which they had heard were true. This book is called *The Gospel According to Luke. Gospel* means "good news." Luke wrote good news about Jesus. What he wrote is the Word of God. The stories in this unit are from the book that Luke wrote.

In the days when Herod was king in Judea, there lived a priest named Zacharias. He and his wife, Elisabeth, were both righteous people. They obeyed God in everything. At this time they were old, and they did not have any children.

Since Zacharias was a priest, he often helped

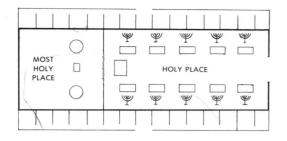

in the worship services at the temple. Besides Zacharias, there were many other priests who helped in the temple. They took turns. For a while one group of priests would do the work that needed to be done at the temple in Jerusalem. Then they would go home, and another group of priests would come and take their place.

Early every morning, before it was sunlight, the priests came to the temple. They needed to get ready for the worship services that day. Some of the priests cleaned away the ashes at the altar where the offerings had been burned the day before. They put more wood on the fire. They were never to let the fire go out. Other priests worked in the room called the holy place. They trimmed the lamps of the ten golden candlesticks. They cleaned the golden altar, where sweet-smelling incense was burned. They put loaves of fresh bread upon the ten tables. Each priest had his own work to do.

131

At nine o'clock in the morning and at three o'clock in the afternoon, the priests offered a lamb on the altar of burnt offering. They also burned incense on the golden altar in the holy place. The people worshiped outside the holy place while a priest offered the incense. Only the priests were allowed to go into the holy place. These two times each day, when the lambs were offered and the incense burned, were called the hours of prayer.

One day while Zacharias burned incense and the people prayed outside the holy place, Zacharias saw God's angel. He was standing on the right side of the altar of incense. Zacharias was much troubled and afraid when he saw the angel.

The angel said to him, "Do not be afraid, Zacharias, for your prayer is heard. Your wife, Elisabeth, will have a son. You shall name him John. You will be very happy, and many people will rejoice when he is born. He shall not drink any wine or strong drink. He shall be filled with God's Spirit from the time that he is born. He shall help many people in Israel to repent of their sins and to obey God."

Zacharias could hardly believe these words. He and his wife were old. How could they have children any more? Zacharias asked the angel, "How can I know that this will happen?"

The angel said to Zacharias, "I am Gabriel, who stands before God. I was sent to tell you this good news. You will be dumb, not able to speak, until this happens, because you did not believe what I said."

Because of his visit with the angel, Zacharias was in the holy place longer than usual. The people outside wondered why he stayed inside so long. When he finally did come out, he could not talk to them. He was dumb, as the angel had said. However, Zacharias made signs to them with his hands. By these signs he was able to make the people understand that he had seen something very unusual.

When Zacharias was finished with his work at the temple, he went home to his wife, Elisabeth.

Lesson 2

The Birth of Jesus Is Announced

Luke 1:26-80

Three months before Baby John was born to Zacharias and Elisabeth, God sent the angel Gabriel to earth with another message. This time he was sent to Elisabeth's cousin Mary. She lived in the city of Nazareth in Galilee. Galilee was a country north of Judea, the home of Zacharias and Elisabeth.

Mary was a young woman, not yet married. But she was engaged to be married to a man named Joseph. Both Joseph and Mary came from the family line of David.

The angel Gabriel came to Mary and said, "Hail! You are well beloved. The Lord is with you. Blessed are you among women."

When Mary saw the angel, she was troubled. She wondered what kind of greeting this was.

The angel said to her, "Do not be afraid, Mary, for you have found favor with God. You shall have a son and shall call His name Jesus. He shall be great and shall be called the Son of the Highest.

134

The Lord shall give Him the throne of His father David. He shall reign over the house of Jacob forever, and His kingdom shall never end."

Mary did not understand how this could be, so the angel explained to her. He said, "The Holy Ghost shall come upon you, and the power of the Highest shall overshadow you. The Holy One who shall be born to you will be the Son of God. Your cousin Elisabeth will also have a son, though she is very old, for with God nothing shall be impossible."

Mary was humble. She was ready to believe what the Lord had told her. She was ready to accept whatever He had for her. She said, "Behold the handmaid of the Lord. Let it be as you have said." Then the angel left her.

Soon after this, Mary went to visit Elisabeth. She hurried to the hill country of Judea, entered the house of Zacharias, and greeted Elisabeth.

When Elisabeth heard Mary's greeting, she was filled with the Holy Ghost. With a loud voice she said to Mary, "Blessed are you among women, and blessed is the One to be born to you. How is this that the mother of my Lord should come to me? Blessed is she who believed, for it shall be done to her as the Lord has said."

Mary said, "My soul magnifies the Lord, and my spirit has rejoiced in God my Saviour. He has seen how lowly I am. From this time on, all generations shall call me blessed. He who is mighty has done great things to me, and holy is His Name. His mercy is on those who fear Him from generation to generation. He has shown strength with His arm. He has scattered the proud in the imagination of their hearts. He has put down the mighty from their seats and lifted up the humble. He has filled the hungry with good things and has sent the rich away empty. He has helped Israel because He remembered His mercy, as he said to our fathers—to Abraham and to his children forever."

Mary stayed with Elisabeth for about three months. Then she returned to her home. This was the time that God gave Elisabeth a son. How happy her friends and neighbors were for Elisabeth! They heard how the Lord had shown mercy to her in giving her a son, and they rejoiced with her.

When the baby was eight days old, the relatives and neighbors gathered together to name the baby. They thought that he should be called Zacharias, after the name of his father. But

Elisabeth said, "No, he shall be called John."

The relatives could not understand this. In those days people usually named their children the same name as one of their relatives. They said to Elisabeth, "None of your relatives are called by this name." They made signs to the baby's father. They wanted to know what he wanted his son to be called. Would he not want his son to have his name or the name of a relative?

Zacharias still could not speak, but he made it known that he wanted a writing tablet. Then he wrote, "His name is John."

Everyone wondered at this. Immediately the mouth of Zacharias was opened, and his tongue was loosed so that he could speak. Zacharias praised God.

The people of the neighborhood feared when they heard these things. Unusual things were happening in their land. Soon people farther away were also hearing about these things. They asked, "What kind of child shall this be?"

The child, John, grew and became strong in spirit. He was in the deserts until the time that God wanted him to show himself to His people Israel.

Jesus Is Born

Luke 2:1-40

At this time Caesar Augustus ruled the world. He made a decree that all the world should be taxed. Everyone went to his own city to be taxed. Because Joseph and Mary were from the family line of David, they needed to go to Bethlehem to be taxed. From their home at Nazareth in Galilee to Bethlehem in Judea was about one hundred miles. They had to travel several days to get to Bethlehem.

While Joseph and Mary were in Bethlehem, Baby Jesus was born. This was God's time and God's place for Jesus to be born. It was written in the Old Testament that Jesus would be born in Bethlehem.

Mary wrapped Baby Jesus in swaddling clothes. She laid Him in a manger because there was no room for them in the inn, where travelers often slept. Bethlehem was crowded at this time. Many people had come to this town to be taxed.

In the same country of Judea, near

Bethlehem, shepherds were watching their flocks of sheep. The night when Jesus was born, the angel of the Lord came to them. The glory of the Lord shone around them. The shepherds were very much afraid.

The angel said to them, "Do not be afraid, for I bring you good tidings of great joy, which shall be to all people. For to you is born this day in the city of David a Saviour, which is Christ the Lord. This shall be a sign to you. You will find the Babe wrapped in swaddling clothes, lying in a manger."

Suddenly there was with the angel a multitude of the heavenly host. They were praising God and saying, "Glory to God in the highest, and on earth peace, good will to men."

After this the angels disappeared into heaven. Then the shepherds said to one another, "Let us now go to Bethlehem and see this thing which is come to pass, which the Lord has made known to us."

They hurried to Bethlehem. There they found Mary and Joseph and the baby. The baby was wrapped in swaddling clothes and lying in a manger. Everything was just as the angel had told them it would be.

After the shepherds had seen Jesus, they

spread far and wide the tidings that the angel had told them about Jesus. It was good news for all people. Everyone who heard it wondered about the things the shepherds told them.

The shepherds returned to their flocks. They glorified and praised God for all the things they had heard and seen just as it had been told to them.

Eight days after Jesus was born, He was named, as Baby John had been. It was the custom in those days to name a baby on the eighth day. Both John and Jesus had their names chosen before they were born. The angel Gabriel had told the parents of both what their babies should be named. Yet they were named on the eighth day according to the custom in those days.

Some days after this, Joseph and Mary took Baby Jesus to the temple at Jerusalem. They went to present Him to the Lord. In the Old Testament Law it was written that this should be done with the first-born son. The Law required a sacrifice of a pair of turtledoves or two young pigeons. Joseph and Mary offered this sacrifice according to God's Law.

At this time there was at Jerusalem a godly man whose name was Simeon. The Holy Ghost had revealed to Simeon that he would not die before he saw the Christ. So he was waiting for Jesus to come. Simeon came by the Spirit into the temple. He was there when Joseph and Mary brought in the child Jesus to do with Him as the Law said. Simeon took Jesus up into his arms and blessed God. Then he prayed, "Lord, now let Your servant depart in peace, according to Your word; for my eyes have seen Your salvation, which You have prepared before the face of all people—a light to lighten the Gentiles, and the glory of Your people Israel."

Joseph and Mary marveled at the things that Simeon said about Jesus. Truly they were wonderful words.

Simeon blessed Joseph and Mary also. He said to Mary, "This child is set for the fall and rising again of many in Israel. He is set for a sign which shall be spoken against. Yes, a sword shall pierce through your own soul also, that the thoughts of many hearts may be made known."

There was also at the temple a very old woman of God. Her name was Anna. She had lived with her husband only seven years before he died, leaving her a widow. She had now been a widow for many years. She stayed in the temple, serving

142

God with fastings and prayers night and day. At that instant, she came to Joseph and Mary and thanked God. She spoke of Jesus to all those in Jerusalem who were looking for God's salvation.

Joseph and Mary did all things according to the Law of the Lord. Then they returned to Galilee to their own city Nazareth. The child Jesus grew and became strong in spirit. He was filled with wisdom, and the grace of God was upon Him.

Lesson 4

The Early Life of Jesus and John
Luke 2:41–3:18

Every year Joseph and Mary went to the feast of the Passover at Jerusalem. When Jesus was twelve years old, they again went to Jerusalem for this feast. It lasted for seven days.

After the feast, as the people traveled toward home, Jesus was not with Joseph and Mary. They thought He was somewhere in the crowd of travelers. After they had traveled a whole day, they looked for Him among their relatives and friends, but they could not find Him. Now they realized that He was missing.

Joseph and Mary would not go home without Jesus. They turned back to Jerusalem to look for Him there. After three days they found Him. He was in the temple, sitting with the Jewish leaders. He was listening to what they had to say. He was also asking them questions. The people who heard the things Jesus said were surprised at His understanding. He gave answers that showed He understood the Bible very well although He was

144

only twelve years old.

When Joseph and Mary saw Jesus in the temple, they were amazed. Jesus did not seem to be afraid because He was left behind. He was not disturbed because He had not seen His parents for several days.

His mother said to Him, "Son, why have You done this? See, Your father and I have looked for You sorrowing." Yes, three days was a long time for His mother not to know where her Son was. She and Joseph were in sorrow, not knowing what had happened to Him.

Jesus asked, "Why have you been searching for Me? Did you not know that I must be about My Father's business?"

Joseph and Mary did not understand what Jesus was talking about. Jesus was thinking about His Father in heaven. He was thinking about what His heavenly Father wanted Him to do. He wanted to obey Him. He also wanted to obey His earthly parents, because that is God's will for children. So He went along home with them to Nazareth. He submitted to them and did what they wanted Him to do. God had commanded, "Honour thy father and thy mother."

Jesus grew in wisdom. He grew in stature. He also grew in favor with God and with man.

While Jesus was growing up, John was in the wilderness of Judea. But the time came that God wanted John to leave the wilderness and show himself to Israel. God wanted him to preach and to baptize people who were truly sorry for their sins. Because he baptized, he was known as John the Baptist. It would soon be time for Jesus to begin His work of preaching and teaching among the people. John the Baptist was to prepare the people to listen to Jesus.

John left the wilderness and came into the country around the Jordan River. He preached, saying, "Repent, for the kingdom of heaven is at hand."

Many people came to John to be baptized. But some who came were not ready to be baptized. They had not repented of their sins. They did not think that they needed to repent of any sin. They thought that because they were descendants of faithful Abraham, they were good people.

John could not baptize them until they knew that they were sinners and repented of their sins. He said to the people, "Show that you have repented of your sins." How do people show that

146

they have repented of their sins? First, they must confess their sins. Then they must stop doing those wrong things.

John warned the people, "Do not think that you are all right because Abraham is your father. God is able to take these stones and raise up children to Abraham from them."

John the Baptist compared the people to trees. He said, "The ax is now laid to the root of the trees. Every tree that does not bring forth good fruit is cut down and thrown into the fire."

The people were concerned about themselves. If they did not show that they had repented of their sins, they would be cut down. They would have no right to go to heaven. They would be cast into hellfire. This was serious. They asked John, "What shall we do then?"

John answered, "Whoever has two coats, let him give one of them to someone who has no coat. He who has food, let him do the same."

When the tax collectors came to be baptized, they also asked, "Master, what shall we do?"

John said to them, "Do not ask for more money from the people than you have been told to charge them."

The soldiers asked John, "And what shall we

do?''

John said to them, "Do not harm anyone. Neither shall you accuse anyone of something that is not true; and be content with your wages.''

The people were wondering, "Who is this strange preacher? Is this the Christ, or not?''

John said to them, "I indeed baptize you with water. But One mightier than I is coming. I am not worthy to untie His shoestring. He shall baptize you with the Holy Ghost and with fire. His fan is in His hand, and He will thoroughly clean His floor. He will gather the wheat into His storehouse, but He will burn up the chaff with fire that cannot be put out.'' John also preached many other things to the people.

Jesus Is Tempted

Luke 3:19–4:32

While John was baptizing, Jesus came down from Galilee and was baptized by John. After Jesus was baptized, and while He was praying, the heaven was opened. The Holy Spirit came down from heaven in the shape of a dove and lighted on Jesus. A voice from heaven said, "You are My beloved Son; in You I am well pleased."

Jesus was about thirty years old at this time. Now Jesus, being full of the Holy Spirit, was led by the Spirit into the wilderness. For forty days He was in the wilderness, tempted of the devil. During those forty days, He ate nothing. So when the forty days were ended, He was hungry.

The devil said to Jesus, "If You are the Son of God, command this stone to be made into bread."

Jesus answered him, "It is written that man shall not live by bread alone, but by every word of God."

The devil took Him up into a high mountain.

He showed Him all the kingdoms of the world in a moment of time. The devil said to Him, "I will give You all this power and the glory of these kingdoms because it is given to me. And I give it to whomever I wish. If You will worship me, all shall be Yours."

Jesus answered, "Get behind Me, Satan, because it is written, 'You shall worship the Lord your God, and Him only shall you serve.'"

The devil brought Jesus to Jerusalem. He set Him on a high point on the temple. He said, "If You are the Son of God, throw Yourself down from here, because it is written, 'He shall give His angels charge over you to keep you. And in their hands they shall hold you up, lest at any time you dash your foot against a stone.'"

Jesus answered, "It is said, 'You shall not tempt the Lord your God.'"

When the devil had finished all these temptations, he departed from Jesus for a while.

About this time Jesus heard that John the Baptist had been thrown into prison. John had said to King Herod, "It is wrong for you to have your brother Philip's wife." He had also told Herod about many other evils that he had done. Because of this King Herod had John put into prison. When Jesus heard that John was put into prison, He returned to Galilee in the power of the Spirit.

Many people in Galilee heard of Jesus and of the wonderful things that He could do. He taught them in their synagogues, and they praised Him.

Jesus came to Nazareth, where He had been brought up. As His custom was, He went into the synagogue on the Sabbath Day and stood up to read. The Book of the prophet Isaiah was given to Him. When He had opened the Book, He found the place where it is written, "The Spirit of the Lord God is upon Me, because He has anointed Me to preach the Gospel to the poor. He has sent Me to heal the brokenhearted; to preach deliverance to the captives, and recovering of sight to the blind; to set at liberty those who are bruised; to preach the acceptable year of the Lord."

Jesus then closed the Book. He gave it again to the minister and sat down. All the people in the synagogue kept looking at Jesus. Jesus began to say to them, "This day this Scripture has come to pass."

Everyone listened to what He said. They wondered about the gracious words that came

151

from His mouth. They knew of no other man who spoke as He did. They said, "Is not this Joseph's son?" How could a son of Joseph speak such wonderful words? They did not know that He is the Son of God.

Jesus said to them, "You will surely tell Me this proverb, 'Doctor, heal Yourself. What we have heard that You did in Capernaum, do also here in Your own country.' Verily I say to you, no prophet is accepted in his own country. But I tell you truthfully that many widows were in Israel in the days of Elijah when the heaven was shut up for three years and six months and a great famine was throughout all the land. Elijah was not sent to any of them except to a city of Sidon to a woman who was a widow. Many lepers were in Israel in the time of Elisha the prophet. However, none of them were healed except Naaman the Syrian."

When the people in the synagogue heard these things, they became very angry. They seemed to know that these stories were to show them what they were like. As the people of Israel had not believed that Elijah and Elisha were true prophets, so they did not believe that Jesus is the Son of God.

As in the time of Elijah no widow in Israel would take care of Elijah, so these people would not care for Jesus. And no leper except Naaman, a stranger, had come to Elisha to be healed. Jesus knew that these people who had grown up with Him would not come to Him for help either. Neither would they believe Him even if He did miracles there.

In great anger the people of Nazareth got up and forced Jesus out of their city. They led Him to the brow of the hill on which their city was built. They were going to throw Him down headfirst.

But Jesus passed through the middle of them and went on His way. He came down to Capernaum, a city along the Sea of Galilee. There He taught the people on the Sabbath days. The people were astonished at His preaching, because His words were so powerful.

Lesson 6

Jesus Teaches and Heals

Luke 4:33–5:16

In the synagogue at Capernaum was a man who had a spirit of an unclean devil. The spirit cried out with a loud voice. He said to Jesus, "Let us alone. What have we to do with You, Jesus of Nazareth? Have You come to destroy us? I know who You are. You are the Holy One of God."

Jesus said to the devil, "Keep still and come out of him."

When the devil had thrown the man into their midst, he came out of the man and did not hurt him.

All the people were amazed when they saw this. They said among themselves, "What a word is this? With authority and power He commands the unclean spirits, and they come out." In every part of the country around Capernaum Jesus became known for the wonderful things He did.

Jesus went out of the synagogue and came into Simon Peter's house. Peter's wife's mother had a high fever. The people asked Jesus to help

154

her. Jesus stood over her and rebuked the fever. The fever left her, and she immediately got up and served them.

When the sun was setting, everyone who had any sick folks brought them to Jesus. The sick people had many different diseases. Jesus laid His hands on every one of them and healed them. Devils also came out of many. They would cry out and say, "You are Christ, the Son of God." But Jesus would not allow them to speak, because they knew that He was Christ.

The next day Jesus went into a desert place. The people were so eager to see Him that they looked for Him until they found Him. Then they asked Him not to leave them.

Jesus said to them, "I must preach the kingdom of God to other cities also, because that is why I am sent." And this is what He did. He preached in the synagogues of Galilee.

As many people pressed near Jesus to hear the Word of God, He stood by the lake called the Sea of Galilee. There Jesus saw two ships along the shore. The fishermen had gone out of them and were washing their nets. Jesus went into the ship that belonged to Simon Peter. He said to Simon, "Please push the ship out into the water

155

a little way from the land." Then Jesus sat down and taught the people from the ship. That way they could not crowd around Him so closely.

When Jesus was finished speaking to the people, He said to Simon, "Launch out into the deep and let down your nets to catch fish."

Simon answered, "Master, we have worked all night and have caught nothing. Yet, if You tell me to do it, I will let down the net."

So, at the command of Jesus, the fishermen let down the net into the sea. A great multitude of fish were caught in the net. In fact, there were so many that the net broke. The fishermen beckoned to their partners, who were in another ship, to come and help them. Their partners came to take some of the load of fish. But there were so many fish that both ships were filled and began to sink with the heavy load.

When Simon Peter saw what was happening, he fell down before Jesus. He said, "Depart from me, for I am a sinful man, O Lord." He said this because he was so astonished at what had just happened. Everyone was surprised—even James and John, who were partners with Simon. Indeed, this was a miracle. They had been fishing all night and had caught nothing. Now, in one catch, at

Jesus' command, they had two ships so full of fish that they were in danger of sinking.

Jesus said to Simon, "Do not be afraid. From now on, you will catch men." Yes, they would be fishers of men, rescuing people from the sea of sin into the net of the kingdom of God.

When the fishermen came back to land, they left everything to follow Jesus.

As Jesus was in a certain city, He saw a man full of leprosy. When the man saw Jesus, he fell on his face and begged Jesus for help. He said, "Lord, if You will, You can make me clean."

Jesus put out His hand and touched the man. He said, "I will. Be clean."

Immediately his leprosy was gone. Jesus commanded the man, "Do not tell anyone, but go and show yourself to the priest. For a testimony to them, offer for your cleansing what Moses commanded."

Although Jesus told the man to be quiet, more and more people heard about Him. Great multitudes of people came together to listen to Him and to be healed of their sicknesses.

Jesus went away from the people into the wilderness to pray.

People Find Fault With Jesus

Luke 5:17-39

One day as Jesus was teaching, Jewish leaders, called Pharisees, and teachers, called scribes, were there. They had come out of every town of Galilee and Judea and from Jerusalem. The power of God was there to heal people.

Some men brought a bed on which a man lay who had palsy. They looked for a way to bring the sick man inside the house. They wanted to lay him in front of Jesus so that Jesus would heal him. But so many people were crowded in that house they could find no way to get him to Jesus. But they did not give up. They took the sick man up on the roof of the house. The roof was made of tiles. The men took away enough of the tiles to make a hole large enough to let the man down through the hole. Down went the man on his couch through the hole in the tiling. He was lowered until he was down in the crowd in front of Jesus.

Jesus saw that these people believed that He

could heal this man. If they had not believed, they would not have gone to all this work. When Jesus saw their faith, He said to the sick man, "Man, your sins are forgiven."

The scribes and Pharisees began to think about what Jesus said. "Who is this that dares to speak such awful words?" they thought. "Who can forgive sins but God alone?" They thought that Jesus was only a man. They thought that He did not have the right to say that this man's sins were forgiven. They did not know that He is God's Son.

Jesus knew what they were thinking. He asked, "Why are you thinking these things? Which is easier to say, 'Your sins are forgiven,' or 'Rise up and walk'?" Then, so that they could know that Jesus does have power on earth to forgive sins, He said to the sick man, "Arise, and take up your couch, and go into your house."

Immediately the sick man got up from his couch. He took up the couch on which he had been lying, and went to his own house. As he went, he gave glory to God.

Everyone was amazed. They praised the Lord. They were filled with fear, saying, "We have seen strange things today."

After this Jesus went out of the house. He saw a man named Levi sitting at his work. Jesus said to him, "Follow Me."

Immediately the man left everything and got up and followed Jesus. This man was Matthew, the man who wrote the first book in the New Testament. He is also called Levi. Matthew was a publican, or a tax collector.

Matthew made a great feast at his house for Jesus. Many other publicans were with them at the feast. The disciples of Jesus were also there, sitting with the publicans at the feast.

The scribes and Pharisees found fault with Jesus' disciples. They asked the disciples, "Why do you eat and drink with publicans and sinners?"

That was something that the scribes and Pharisees would not do. They would not eat with publicans. Publicans were sinners! The scribes and Pharisees did not think that they themselves were sinners.

The publicans were a despised group of people. They were often dishonest, and made the people pay more tax than they were told to collect. They kept this extra money for themselves to make themselves rich.

The scribes and Pharisees looked upon the

publicans as being among the worst of sinners. The Pharisees were the strictest group among the Jews. They claimed to obey all the teachings of the Old Testament. But they were hypocrites, for they only pretended to obey the Law. Jesus said of them, "Everything they do is to be seen of men." They did not do things to please God. They looked down on people who did not do as they said. The scribes were Jewish writers and teachers. They copied the Law and taught the people from the Scriptures. The scribes worked with the Pharisees, and many of them were also hypocrites.

So when the scribes and Pharisees asked Jesus' disciples, "Why do you eat with publicans and sinners?" Jesus answered them. He said, "I came to help sinners." Jesus could help people who knew they were sinners. They welcomed His help. Jesus could not help those who did not know they were sinners. They did not think they needed His help.

Then the scribes and Pharisees asked Jesus, "Why do the disciples of John the Baptist fast? And why do the disciples of the Pharisees often fast and pray, but Your disciples eat and drink?" The Pharisees thought they were better than the disciples of Jesus, because they fasted and prayed. But they did not fast and pray for a good reason. They did this only to get praise from men.

Jesus had a good answer for their question. He said, "When I go away to heaven, My disciples will fast. It is not yet time for them to fast." To help them understand this, He said, "No man puts a piece of a new garment in an old garment. The new piece would make the old piece tear worse. The new and the old do not go together." Jesus also said, "No man puts new wine into old bottles because the new wine would break the old bottles. No one who has drunk old wine wants new wine, because he says, 'The old is better.' "

Lesson 8

Great Teachings of Jesus

Luke 6:1-26

One Sabbath Day Jesus walked through the grain field with His disciples. As they walked along, the disciples picked some of the grain. They rubbed it in their hands and ate it.

The Pharisees asked, "Why do Your disciples do this? According to the Law, it is not right to pick grain on the Sabbath Day."

Jesus asked them, "Have you never read what David did when he and the men who were with him were hungry? He went into the house of God and ate the bread that only the priests were supposed to eat. He gave some of it to the men who were with him, and they also ate. The Son of Man is Lord also of the Sabbath Day."

On another Sabbath Day, Jesus went into the synagogue and taught the people. A man who had a withered hand was there. The scribes and Pharisees were watching Jesus to see whether He would heal this man on the Sabbath Day. They did not like Jesus. They wanted to find fault with

163

Him. But they could not rightly find fault with Him, because He only did good things.

Jesus knew that the scribes and Pharisees were watching Him. He knew what they were thinking. That would not stop Him from doing right. He said to the man who had the withered hand, "Get up and stand out in the middle. The man obeyed. Then Jesus asked the scribes and Pharisees, "Is it right to do good or to do evil on the Sabbath days? Is it right to save life, or to destroy it?"

As Jesus looked around upon them all, He said to the man, "Stretch out your hand." The man stretched out his hand. It was made well again just like the other hand.

When the scribes and Pharisees saw this, they were filled with madness. Here was Someone who did not agree with them. Yet He could do such great and wonderful things. They wanted to get rid of Him. They talked among themselves. They asked one another, "How can we get rid of Him?"

Jesus left the synagogue and went out into a mountain to pray. All night long He prayed to God. The next day He called His disciples. Of His disciples, He chose twelve men whom He called apostles. Their names were Simon (whom He also called Peter) and Andrew his brother, James and John, Philip and Bartholomew, Matthew and Thomas, James the son of Alphaeus, another Simon, Judas the brother of James, and Judas who betrayed Jesus.

Jesus came down with them and stood in the plain. Many of His disciples and a great multitude of people came to Jesus there. These people were from Judea and Jerusalem and from the seacoast of Tyre and Sidon. They came to hear Jesus and to be healed of their diseases. Others who were troubled with unclean spirits came also, and they were healed. Everyone wanted to touch Him because power went out from Him to heal them all.

Jesus looked upon His disciples. They were not like the Pharisees who thought they were righteous. They knew that they were poor sinners who needed Jesus. That is why they had been willing to leave everything to follow Him. Jesus said to them, "Blessed are you poor, for yours is the kingdom of God. Blessed are you who hunger now, for you shall be filled." Yes, the disciples were hungry for the kind words of comfort and hope that Jesus alone could give to them. The scribes and Pharisees were satisfied with themselves.

Jesus continued to comfort His disciples. He said, "Blessed are you who weep now, for you shall laugh." The disciples wept and were sorry for their sins. Sometime they would be filled with joy in heaven. Jesus' kind words comforted them.

Jesus had more kind words for them because they were willing to suffer for His sake. He said, "Blessed are you when men shall hate you. Blessed are you when they shall separate you from their company. Blessed are you when they shall reproach you for the Son of Man's sake. Rejoice in that day. Leap for joy, for your reward is great in heaven. That is the way their fathers did to the prophets."

Jesus had words of woe for the scribes and Pharisees. He said, "Woe to you who are rich. You have received your comfort." Yes, they had received comfort from having men know that they gave much money. They had so much money that they could give much and still have a lot left for themselves. God was not pleased with their giving.

Jesus said to them also, "Woe to you who are full! For you shall hunger. Woe to you who laugh now! For you shall mourn and weep. Woe to you

166

when all men shall speak well of you! That is the way your fathers did to the false prophets."

How truly Jesus spoke! False prophets had lied to the Jews. And the Jews had loved to hear the things they said.

Lesson 9

More Great Teachings of Jesus

Luke 6:27-49

Jesus taught His followers to love their enemies. He said, "Do good to those who hate you. Bless those who curse you. Pray for those who are mean to you. If anyone hits you on one cheek, offer to let him hit you on your other cheek, too. If anyone takes away one of your coats, let him have your other coat, too. If someone asks you for something, give it to him. If anyone steals anything from you, do not ask him for it again."

Jesus taught the Golden Rule. He said, "As ye would that men should do to you, do ye also to them likewise." He explained, "If you love only the people who love you, you are no different from sinners. Even sinners love those who love them. If you do good only to those who do good to you, you are no better than sinners. Sinners also do that much. If you lend things only to those who lend to you or give back what they borrowed, you are not better than sinners. Sinners also loan things to others if they think that they will receive again as much as they loaned. Love your enemies, do good, and lend without hoping to receive anything back. Then your reward shall be great. You will be the children of God, doing like your Father in heaven. He is kind to the unthankful and the evil people. He shows mercy to others who are in need."

Jesus taught, "Judge not, and you shall not be judged. Condemn not, and you shall not be condemned. Forgive, and you shall be forgiven." He wanted His disciples to understand that they could not help others until they realized they were sinners and God helped them. He asked, "Can the blind lead the blind? Will they not both fall into the ditch? How can you say to a brother, 'Let me pull out the mote that is in your eye,' when there is a beam in your own eye? First take care of the beam in your own eye, then you can see clearly to help your brother."

Jesus said, "A good tree does not bring forth evil fruit; neither does an evil tree bring forth good fruit. Every tree is known by its own fruit. Men do not gather figs from thorns or grapes from a bramble." That is how it is with men. A good man who has a good heart does good things. He speaks right words. But an evil man who has an evil he does bad things and speaks bad words.

Jesus asked the evil people, "Why do you call Me, 'Lord, Lord,' and yet do not the things that I say?" He told a story to show the difference between people who obey Him and people who only pretend to obey Him. He said, "Whoever comes to Me and hears what I say, and does what I say, I will show you whom he is like. He is like a man who built a house. He digged deep and laid the foundation on a rock. And when the flood arose, the stream beat fiercely upon that house. But the water could not shake the house, for it was built on a rock. But he that hears what I say and does not do it is like a man that built a house on the ground without a foundation. The stream beat fiercely against this house, and immediately it fell. And the ruin of that house was great."

Jesus Heals the Ruler's Servant

Luke 7:1-35

When Jesus was finished teaching the people, He went to Capernaum again. At Capernaum there was a Roman ruler who had a servant whom he loved very dearly. This servant was very sick. He was about to die. When the ruler heard about Jesus, he sent some of the older men of the Jews to Jesus. He wanted them to ask Jesus to please come and heal his servant.

When the Jewish men came to Jesus, they begged Him to come. They said, "This ruler is worthy of help because he loves our people. He has even built a synagogue for us."

Jesus went with the men. When Jesus was not very far from the house, the Roman ruler sent friends to Jesus with this message: "Lord, do not trouble Yourself, because I am not worthy that You should enter under my roof. I did not feel worthy myself to come to You, but say the word, and my servant shall be healed. I also am a man under authority and have soldiers under me. I say

171

to one, 'Go,' and he goes. I say to another, 'Come,' and he comes. I say to my servant, 'Do this,' and he does it.''

When Jesus heard this, He marveled. What a humble mind this ruler showed! What faith he had! He showed that he believed in Jesus' power and greatness. Although he was a ruler and had servants, he felt unworthy of Jesus' presence. How different he was from the Pharisees! They had a better opportunity to believe in Jesus than this Roman. They were Jews and had the Old Testament Scriptures that told about Jesus. Jesus turned and said to the people who followed Him, "I say to you, I have not found so great faith; no, not in Israel.''

The men who had been sent to deliver the ruler's message to Jesus returned to the ruler's house. They found his sick servant, not dead, but well!

The next day Jesus went to a city called Nain. Many of His disciples and other people went along with Him. When Jesus came near to the gate of the city, He saw a dead man being carried out. He was the only son of his mother, and she was a widow. Many people of the city were with the woman whose only son had died. When Jesus saw the sorrowing mother, He pitied her greatly. He said to her, "Do not weep."

Jesus touched the bier, and the men who were carrying it stood still. Jesus said to the dead man, "Young man, I say to you, arise!"

The man who was dead sat up. He began to speak. Then Jesus gave him to his mother.

Great fear came on all the people when they saw this, and they gave glory to God. They said, "A great Prophet has come among us. God has visited His people." This saying went throughout all Judea and the country around it.

At this time, John the Baptist was in prison. His disciples went to him. They told him about the wonderful works of Jesus. John wondered if this Jesus was the Christ. He sent two of his followers to Jesus to ask Him, "Are You the One that should come, or do we look for another?"

The men went to Jesus. They said, "John the Baptist has sent us to You. He wants us to ask You, "Are You the One who was to come, or are we to look for another?"

In the same hour that they asked this question, Jesus cured many people of their sicknesses and ailments. He cast out evil spirits. He made blind men see again. Then Jesus said to the men,

"Go your way. Tell John the things which you have seen and heard. The blind see. The lame walk. The lepers are healed. The deaf hear. The dead are raised. The Gospel is preached to the poor. Blessed is everyone who is not offended in Me."

When the messengers left to go to John and tell him what Jesus said, Jesus began to speak to the people about John. He said, "John is the man about whom it is written in the Old Testament, 'Behold, I send my messenger before your face, which shall prepare the way before you.'" Jesus let them know that John was indeed a great prophet.

All the people that heard Jesus believed in God. They had been baptized by John. But the Pharisees and other leaders would not have anything to do with God's words. They had not been baptized by John because they had not repented of their sins. They did not believe that John had come to prepare the way for Jesus. Neither did they believe the teachings of Jesus.

Jesus said, "To what shall I compare the men of this generation, and what are they like? They are like children sitting in the marketplace and calling to one another, saying, 'We have piped to

174

you, and you have not danced. We have mourned to you, and you have not wept.' John the Baptist came neither eating bread nor drinking wine, and you say, 'He has a devil.' The Son of Man is come eating and drinking, and you say, 'See, He is a gluttonous man and a winebibber. He is a friend of publicans and sinners!' "

Yes, they were hard to please. No matter what the people of God did, they found fault with them.

Lesson 11

Jesus Visits in Simon's Home

Luke 7:36–8:21

A Pharisee named Simon invited Jesus to come and eat with him. Jesus accepted the invitation. He went into Simon's house and sat down to eat.

In the same city there was a woman who was known to be a sinner. When she knew that Jesus was eating at the Pharisee's house, she came, bringing a box of ointment. She stood behind Jesus at His feet, weeping, and began to wash His feet with her tears. She wiped them with the hairs of her head. She kissed His feet and anointed them with the ointment.

When Simon saw it, he thought, "If this man were a prophet, He would know what kind of woman is touching Him."

Jesus knew what Simon was thinking. He said to him, "Simon, I have something to say to you."

Simon answered, "Master, say on."

Jesus said, "There was a certain man who had two men that owed him money. The one man owed

176

him five hundred pence. The other man owed him fifty pence. When they had nothing to pay, he frankly forgave them both. Tell Me, which of them will love him most?"

Simon said, "I suppose the man who was forgiven the most."

Jesus answered, "You have judged rightly." He turned to the woman and said to Simon, "Do you see this woman? I entered into your house. You gave Me no water for My feet. But she has washed My feet with tears and wiped them with the hair of her head. You gave Me no kiss. But this woman, since the time I came in, has not stopped kissing My feet. You did not anoint My head with oil, but this woman has anointed My feet with ointment. Wherefore I say to you that her sins, which are many, are forgiven because she loved much. But to whom little is forgiven, that person loves little."

Jesus said to the woman, "Your sins are forgiven."

The people who were eating with Jesus wondered at this. They thought, "Who is this who forgives sins also?"

Jesus said to the woman, "Your faith has saved you. Go in peace."

The Pharisee was wrong in thinking that Jesus did not know what kind of woman touched Him. Jesus knew, and even said, that her sins were many. But Jesus knew also that she was sorry for her sins and believed that Jesus would forgive her. Jesus came to help such people.

Jesus knew that Simon also had many sins. But Simon did not see how sinful he was. Therefore he did not confess his sins. He was not sorry for them as the woman was. Neither did he love Jesus as the woman did.

After this Jesus went throughout every city and village, preaching and showing the good news of the kingdom of God. The twelve apostles were with Him. There were also with Him some women who gave of their own things to supply Jesus' needs. Among them were Joanna, Susanna, and Mary Magdalene, out of whom Jesus had cast seven devils.

When many people had gathered to Jesus out of every city, He told them a story, called a parable. He said, "A sower went out to sow seed. As he sowed, some seed fell by the side of the path. It was trodden down, and the birds of the air ate it. Some seed fell upon a rock. As soon as it had sprung up, it withered away because it lacked moisture. Some seed fell among thorns. The thorns sprang up with it and choked it. Other seed fell on good ground. It sprang up and bore fruit—one hundred times as much."

When Jesus had finished this parable, He cried, "He who has ears to hear, let him hear."

His disciples asked Him, "What does this parable mean?"

Jesus said, "I want you to know the mysteries of the kingdom of God. But I speak in parables so that others cannot understand." Jesus did not want others to understand, because they would not believe and obey Him even if they did understand.

But to His disciples who would obey, Jesus explained the meaning of the parable. He said, "The parable is this: The seed is the Word of God. Those by the side of the path are the people who hear. But the devil comes and takes away the Word out of their hearts so that they will not believe and be saved. They on the rock are they who, when they hear, receive the Word with joy. These believe for a while, but they have no root. In time of temptation, they fall away. That which fell among thorns are they who, when they have heard, are choked with the cares and riches and

179

pleasures of this life. They bring forth no fruit to perfection. That which fell on the good ground are those with an honest and a good heart. They, having heard the Word, keep it. They bring forth fruit with patience."

Jesus said, "Give careful attention to how you hear." Those who hear with a desire to understand and obey will be given more understanding. But those who will not do what they hear will lose the understanding they do have.

Jesus' mother and His brothers wanted to come to Jesus. But they could not get to Him because so many others crowded around Him. Some people came to Jesus and said, "Your mother and brothers are standing outside. They want to see You."

Jesus said to them, "My mother and My brothers are those who hear the Word of God and do it."

Lesson 12

Jesus Calms and Heals

Luke 8:22-56

On a certain day Jesus went into a ship with His disciples. He said to them, "Let us go over to the other side of the lake." They launched the ship out onto the lake. As they sailed, Jesus fell asleep. While He slept, a storm of wind swept down upon the lake. The waves tossed high, and the boat was filled with water. Their lives were in danger.

The disciples came to Jesus and awoke Him, saying, "Master, Master, we perish!"

Jesus arose. He rebuked the wind and the water. His word had power. The wind stopped blowing, and the raging sea became calm.

Jesus asked the disciples, "Where is your faith?"

The disciples were afraid. They said to one another, "What kind of man is this! He commands even the winds and the water, and they obey Him."

At last they arrived at the other side of the

lake. They were now in the country of the Gadarenes. When Jesus went onto the land, there met Him from the city a man who had had devils in him for a long time. The man was not in his right mind. He did not wear any clothes. He did not live in a house. He lived in the tombs, where dead people were buried.

Many times a wicked spirit had caught this man. People had tied the man with chains, but they could not keep him bound. The man broke the chains, and then the devil drove him into the wilderness. Jesus came to set such people free from the bondage of Satan. He commanded the unclean spirit, "Come out of the man."

When the man saw Jesus, he fell down before Him. He cried with a loud voice, "What have I to do with You, Jesus, Son of God most high? I beg You not to torment me."

"What is your name?" asked Jesus.

"Legion," answered the man. He said this because many devils were entered into him. *Legion* means "many."

The devils said to Jesus, "Do not command us to go into the pit." Now there was a herd of many pigs feeding on the mountain. The devils said to Jesus, "Allow us to go into these pigs."

Jesus gave them permission to do this. The devils went out of the man and entered into the pigs. The whole herd of pigs ran violently down a steep place into the lake and were drowned.

When the people who fed pigs saw what had happened, they ran away. They told the people in the city and in the country what had happened.

The people went out to see for themselves. They came to Jesus and found the man out of whom the devils had departed. He was sitting at the feet of Jesus. He was dressed in clothes, and he was in his right mind. The people were afraid.

Then the men who had seen what had happened told them how this man was healed.

The whole multitude of people asked Jesus to leave, because they were afraid. They had never heard of such a thing happening before. Jesus went back across the sea into Galilee.

The man out of whom Jesus had cast the devils wanted to be with Jesus. But Jesus said, "Return to your own house. Tell them about the great things that the Lord has done for you."

The man went his way. He published throughout the whole city the great things that the Lord had done for him.

When Jesus returned to Galilee, the people

were waiting for Him and received Him.

Jairus, a ruler of the synagogue, came to Jesus. He fell down at Jesus' feet and said, "Please come to my house." His only daughter, who was about twelve years old, was dying.

As Jesus was on the way to his house, the people crowded around Him. In this crowd was a woman who had had a disease for twelve years. She had spent all her living on doctors, but none of them could heal her. Yet she believed that Jesus could heal her. She came behind Him and touched the border of His garment. Immediately she was healed.

Jesus asked, "Who touched Me?" Everyone denied that he had touched Jesus.

Peter and others who were with Him said, "Master, the multitude crowds around You and presses You. And do You ask, 'Who touched Me?' "

Jesus answered, "Somebody has touched Me. I know that power has gone out of Me."

When the woman saw that she was not hidden, she came trembling. She fell down before Jesus. Before all the people she told Jesus why she had touched Him. She said that she had been healed immediately.

Jesus said to the woman, "Daughter, be of good comfort. Your faith has made you well. Go in peace."

While Jesus was still speaking, a man came from the house of Jairus. He said to Jairus, "Your daughter is dead. Do not trouble the Master."

When Jesus heard it, He comforted Jairus, saying, "Do not be afraid. Only believe, and she shall be made well."

When Jesus came into the house, He would not allow anyone to go into the room except Peter, James, and John, and the father and mother of the girl.

All the people wept and sorrowed because of her death. Jesus said, "Do not weep. She is not dead, but sleeping."

The people laughed and made fun of Jesus for saying that because they knew that the girl was dead. Jesus made them all go out. He took the girl by the hand. He called to her, "Maid, arise."

Her spirit came into her again. Immediately she got up. Jesus commanded that they give her something to eat. Her parents were astonished at what had happened. But Jesus said to them, "Do not tell anyone what has been done."

Lesson 13

Jesus Shows His Power and Glory
Luke 9:1-36

Jesus called His twelve disciples together. He gave them power to cast out all devils and to cure diseases. Then He sent them out to preach the kingdom of God and to heal the sick. He commanded them, "Do not take anything for your journey. Do not take along any food, any extra clothes, or any money to buy food and clothes."

This was different from what most people do when they go on a journey. They usually take food, extra clothes, and money. But Jesus wanted the people to whom He was sending them to feed them and to give them whatever they needed.

Jesus said, "When you come to a city, stay at one place until you leave that city. If the people in the city do not receive you, shake off the dust of your feet against them when you leave the city."

The disciples left. They went through the towns, preaching the Gospel and healing people everywhere.

When King Herod heard all that Jesus had done, he did not know what to think. Some said that He was John the Baptist who had risen from the dead. Herod wondered if this were true. It troubled him because he was the one who had John the Baptist put to death. Some said that the prophet Elijah had appeared again. Others said that one of the old prophets had risen again. Herod said, "I have cut off John's head. But who is this of whom I hear such things?" He wanted to see Jesus.

When the disciples returned from their journey, they told Jesus all the things that they had done. Jesus took them to a desert to be alone with them.

When the other people knew where Jesus had gone, they followed Him. Jesus did not turn them away. He talked to them about the kingdom of God. He healed the ones who needed healing.

Near the close of the day, the twelve apostles came to Jesus. They said, "Send the multitude away that they may go into the towns and country round about and lodge and get food, for we are here in a desert place."

Jesus answered, "You give them something to eat."

They said, "We have nothing more than five loaves and two fishes unless we go and buy food for all these people." Nearly five thousand men were in the crowd. Five loaves and two fishes did not seem even worthwhile to begin feeding the large crowd.

Jesus said to His disciples, "Make the people sit down in groups with fifty in each group."

The disciples did this. All the people sat down in groups of fifty.

Then Jesus took the five loaves and the two fishes. Looking up to heaven, He blessed the food. Then He broke it into pieces and gave it to the disciples to give to the multitude.

All the people ate and were filled, yet there was food left. They gathered together twelve baskets of leftover fragments.

Later when Jesus was praying, His disciples were with Him. Jesus asked them, "Who do the people say that I am?"

They answered, "John the Baptist. But some say Elijah, and others say that one of the old prophets is risen again."

Jesus said to them, "But whom do you say that I am?"

Peter answered, "The Christ of God."

Jesus commanded them, "Do not tell any man." Then Jesus said, "The Son of Man must suffer many things. He will be killed by the elders and the chief priests and scribes. But on the third day He will be raised again."

Jesus told the disciples that whoever wants to follow Him must also be willing to suffer. He must be willing for the sake of Jesus to give up his own self and his own desires. He must be willing to die for Jesus.

Jesus asked them, "What advantage would it be if a man gained the whole world, but lost his own soul?"

Jesus said, "Whoever will be ashamed of Me or of My words, the Son of Man will be ashamed of him when He comes in His own glory and the glory of the Father and of the holy angels. There are some standing here who will not die till they see the kingdom of God."

About eight days after this, Jesus took Peter, James, and John and went up into a mountain to pray. As He prayed, the look on His face changed and His clothes were white and shining. Two men, Moses and Elijah, also appeared in glory. They talked to Jesus about His death at Jerusalem.

Peter, James, and John were very sleepy at

this time. When they woke up, they saw Jesus in His glory and the two men who stood with Him. Peter said to Jesus, "Master, it is good for us to be here. Let us make three tabernacles—one for You, one for Moses, and one for Elijah." Peter said this, not realizing what he was saying.

While he was talking, a cloud came over them, and the disciples were afraid. A voice out of the cloud said, "This is my beloved Son; hear Him." When the voice was still, Jesus was alone with the three disciples again.

The disciples kept these things secret. They did not tell anyone at that time the things which they had seen.

Lesson 14

Jesus Teaches the Disciples

Luke 9:37–10:24

The day after that glorious sight, Jesus, Peter, James, and John came down from the mountain. Many people were there to meet Jesus. One man called to Jesus and said, "Master, I beg You, see my son, because he is my only child. See, a spirit takes him, and he suddenly cries out. It causes him to shake violently, and his mouth foams. It bruises him severely and hardly leaves him. I asked Your disciples to cast him out, but they could not."

Jesus was grieved that His disciples could not cast out the evil spirit. He said to the man, "Bring your son here."

As the boy was coming, the devil threw him down and caused him to shake violently. Jesus made the unclean spirit go out of the boy. He healed the child and gave him back to his father.

Everyone was amazed at the mighty power of God. While they were wondering about the things that Jesus did, Jesus spoke to His

192

disciples. He wanted to prepare them for the time when He would die. He said, "Let these sayings sink into your ears, because the Son of Man shall be delivered into the hands of men."

The disciples did not understand these words, and they were afraid to ask Jesus what He meant. Among themselves they argued about which of them would be the greatest.

Jesus, knowing what they were thinking, took a child and set him beside Him. He said to the disciples, "Whoever shall receive this child in My Name receives Me. Whoever shall receive Me receives Him who sent Me. Whoever will be lowliest among you shall be great."

John said to Jesus, "Master, we saw someone casting out devils in Your Name. We told him not to do it, because he does not follow us."

Jesus answered, "Do not tell him not to do it, because he who is not against us is for us."

When the time came that Jesus must soon go back to heaven, He and His disciples left Galilee. With determination, He set His face to go to Jerusalem, even though He knew that He would be killed there.

Jesus sent messengers on ahead of Him to get ready for Him. To go from Galilee to Judea, they needed to go through Samaria. The disciples came to one of the villages of the Samaritans to get ready for Jesus. But the people there would not receive Jesus because He was going to Jerusalem.

James and John saw that the Samaritans would not receive Jesus. They said, "Lord, do You want us to command fire to come down from heaven and kill them as Elijah did?"

Jesus turned to James and John. He rebuked them for wanting to destroy these people. James and John did not yet understand God's love and ways. Jesus said, "I did not come to destroy men's lives, but to save them."

Since the people in this village would not receive them, they went on to another village. While they were in the way, a man said to Jesus, "Lord, I will follow You wherever You go."

Jesus said, "Foxes have holes. Birds of the air have nests. But the Son of Man has nowhere to lay His head." Yes, the animals have homes, but Jesus did not have even a pillow on which to lay His head. If this man wanted to follow Him wherever He went, he would need to suffer with Him.

Jesus said to another man, "Follow Me."

The man answered, "First allow me to go and

194

bury my father."

Jesus said to him, "Let the dead bury their dead. You go and preach the kingdom of God."

Another man said, "Lord, I will follow You, but first let me go and say good-bye to the people at my house."

Jesus answered, "No man having put his hand to the plow and looking back is fit for the kingdom of God." People who begin to follow Christ, but do not continue to follow, are not fit for heaven.

After this the Lord appointed seventy other men to help in the work of spreading the Gospel. He sent them out in groups of two to the cities where He also would come. He said to them, "The needs are very great, but there are few men to work for Me. Pray to the Lord that more workers might be sent out. Go your ways. Behold, I send you out as lambs among wolves. Carry no purse, food bag, or shoes. Do not salute any man by the way.

"Into whatever house you enter, first say, 'Peace be to this house.' If the son of peace is there, your peace will rest on that house. If not, it shall return to you.

"Into whatever city you enter and they receive you, eat the things that are set before you.

195

Heal the sick who are there. Say to them, 'The kingdom of God has come near you.' But into whatever city you enter and they do not receive you, go out into the street. Say, 'Even the very dust of your city which sticks to us, we wipe off against you. Yet be sure of this, the kingdom of God has come near you.' "

The seventy men went out and did as Jesus had commanded them. Then they returned to Jesus with joy. They said, "Lord, even the devils are subject to us through Your Name."

Jesus said, "I saw Satan as lightning fall from heaven. See, I give you power to walk on snakes and scorpions, and over all the power of the enemy. Nothing shall by any means hurt you. Yet do not rejoice in this. Rather, rejoice because your names are written in heaven."

In that hour Jesus rejoiced in spirit and said, "I thank You, O Father, Lord of heaven and earth, that You have hidden these things from the wise and prudent and have showed them to babes. Even so, Father, for that is what seemed good to You."

The people who thought they were wise and good did not come to Jesus. He could not teach them the wonderful words of God. The people who

196

knew that they were neither wise nor good came to Jesus. He could tell them wonderful things. He could give them power to do His work. Jesus was thankful for this. He was glad that the seventy could understand the things of God and obey Him. He said to them, "Many prophets and kings have wanted to see the things that you are seeing and have not seen them. They have wanted to hear the things that you are hearing and have not heard them."

Lesson 15

Lessons on Love and Prayer

Luke 10:25–11:13

In Jesus' time there were Jews who were experts in knowing God's laws. These men were called lawyers. One of these lawyers stood up to tempt Jesus. He said, "Master, what shall I do to have eternal life?"

Jesus asked him a question to help the lawyer answer his own question. He asked, "What is written in the Law? How do you read?"

The lawyer answered, "You shall love the Lord your God with all your heart, and with all your soul, and with all your strength, and with all your mind. And you shall love your neighbor as yourself."

Jesus said to him, "You have answered right. Do this, and you shall live."

The lawyer was not willing to admit that he had disobeyed this commandment of God. He wanted to believe that he was a righteous man. He wanted others to believe this, too. So he asked Jesus, "And who is my neighbor?"

198

To answer this question, Jesus first told him a story. Then again He asked him a question to help the lawyer answer his own question. He said, "A certain man went from Jerusalem to Jericho. Thieves caught him. They took off his clothes. They wounded him and left him half dead.

"It happened that a priest came down that same road. He saw the man lying there half dead. Then he passed by on the other side of the road.

"A Levite also came by that way. When he saw the man, he went over and looked at him. Then he, too, went by on the other side of the road.

"A certain Samaritan also journeyed down that road. He also came to where the man was. When he saw the wounded man, he felt sorry for him. He went to him and bandaged his wounds, pouring in oil and wine. He put the man on his own animal and brought him to an inn. There he took care of the man. When he left the next day, he gave money to the man in charge of the inn. He said to him, 'Take care of this man. Whatever more you spend for him, I will repay when I come back.' "

Thus Jesus finished His story. Then he asked the man, "Which now of these three men do you think was neighbor to him who fell among the

199

thieves?"

The lawyer answered, "The one who showed mercy on him."

Jesus said, "You go and do the same." Jesus was teaching the lawyer a lesson on love. If we love people, we will help them if we can. Anyone whom we can help or to whom we can show kindness is our neighbor.

As Jesus and His followers were traveling, they came to a village. There a woman named Martha received Jesus into her house. Martha had a sister named Mary. She sat at Jesus' feet and listened to what He had to say. But Martha was very busy—too busy to sit at Jesus' feet and listen to His wonderful words. She was preparing the meal. She did not think it was right for Mary to sit and listen to Jesus and leave her alone to prepare the meal. She came to Jesus and said, "Lord, do You not care that my sister has left me to serve alone? Tell her to help me."

Jesus answered, "Martha, Martha, you are careful and troubled about many things. But one thing is necessary, and Mary has chosen that good part. It shall not be taken away from her."

One time Jesus was praying in a certain place. When He finished, one of His disciples said,

"Lord, teach us to pray, as John also taught his disciples."

Jesus said to them, "When you pray, say, 'Our Father who is in heaven, hallowed be Your Name. Your kingdom come. Your will be done; as in heaven, so in earth. Give us day by day our daily bread, and forgive us our sins; for we also forgive everyone who is indebted to us. And do not lead us into temptation, but deliver us from evil.' "

Jesus wanted His disciples to know that God is pleased when we pray to Him. He said, "Which of you shall have a friend and shall go to him at midnight and say to him, 'Friend, lend me three loaves; a friend of mine in his journey has come to me, and I have nothing to set before him'? The one inside shall answer and say, 'Do not trouble me. The door is now shut, and my children are in bed with me. I cannot rise and give to you.'

"I tell you, though he will not get up and give to him because he is his friend, yet, because he keeps on asking, he will get up and give him as much bread as he needs. I say to you, ask, and it shall be given you. Seek, and you shall find. Knock, and it shall be opened to you. For everyone who asks receives. And he who seeks finds. And to him who knocks, it shall be opened.

"If a son shall ask for bread of any of you who is a father, will he give him a stone? Or if he asks for a fish, will he give him a serpent? Or if he shall ask for an egg, will he offer him a scorpion? If you then, being evil, know how to give good gifts to your children, how much more shall your heavenly Father give the Holy Spirit to those who ask Him?"

Yes, God wants His children to ask Him for whatever they need. He likes to give them good things.

Lesson 16

Jesus Talks to the Hypocrites

Luke 11:14-54

Jesus cast a devil out of a man who was dumb. When the devil was gone out, the man began to speak. The people wondered about this. Some of them said, "Jesus casts out devils by the power of Beelzebub, the chief of the devils." Others tempted Jesus by asking Him for a sign from heaven.

Jesus knew what these people were thinking. He wanted them to see how wrong it is to think that Satan would cast out himself. If he did that, he would be working against himself. Jesus said, "A kingdom divided against itself is brought to ruin." It takes someone stronger than Satan to have power over him. Only the power of God can cast out devils.

But these people were not willing to believe that Jesus is the Son of God. They saw that He did have power over Satan. But they still would not believe in Him, because they did not want to believe Him.

203

Jesus said, "When the unclean spirit goes out of a man, he walks through dry places. He looks for rest, but he can find no rest. He says, 'I will return to the house from which I came.' When he comes back, he finds the house swept and decorated. Then he goes and finds seven other spirits more wicked than himself. They go into the man and live there. Then the man is in a worse condition than he was before."

As Jesus was talking, a certain woman blessed the mother of Jesus for having such a wonderful Son. But Jesus said, "Yes, but rather blessed are those who hear the Word of God and keep it." It is wonderful that everyone who will may be blessed.

When thick crowds gathered together, Jesus told them, "This is an evil generation. They look for a sign, and no sign shall be given to them except the sign of Jonah the prophet. For as Jonah was a sign to the people of Nineveh, so shall I be to this generation.

"The Queen of Sheba shall rise up in judgment and condemn this generation. She came from the farthest part of the earth to hear the wisdom of Solomon; and, see, a greater than Solomon is here.

"The men of Nineveh shall rise up in judgment

204

with this generation. They will condemn it, for they repented at the preaching of Jonah; and, see, a greater than Jonah is here."

It was true. These people would not repent. If they had really wanted to know that Jesus was sent of God, they could have known. They did not need a sign. They simply were not willing to see that they were sinners and that Jesus is righteous. So Jesus did not tell them who He is.

Jesus taught how important it is to do what one knows he should do. If one does not, soon many things that he knows are right will even seem wrong to him.

As Jesus was speaking, a certain Pharisee asked Jesus to eat with him. Jesus went in and sat down to eat. The Pharisee noticed that Jesus had not washed before He ate. He noticed this because the Pharisees were always careful to wash before eating. They thought it was sinful not to wash before eating. So this Pharisee wondered that Jesus did not wash before dinner.

Jesus said to him, "Now you Pharisees make clean the outside of the cup and the platter. But your inward parts are full of greediness and wickedness. You fools, did not He who made the outside make that which is inside also? Give to the poor, and then all things will be clean to you."

But the Pharisees were greedy. They did not like to give their money to the poor. They were mean to the poor and needy. Yes, they were careful to wash themselves and keep the outside of their bodies clean. But inside, their hearts were black with sin. They were greedy and selfish. They did not love the Lord nor the poor sinners whom He came to save.

Jesus said to them, "Woe to you Pharisees! You love the best seats in the synagogues. You love greetings in the markets. Woe to you, scribes and Pharisees, hypocrites! You are like graves which cannot be seen. Men who walk over them do not know that they are there."

One of the lawyers said to Jesus, "Master, by saying this You reproach us also."

Jesus answered, "Woe to you also, you lawyers! For you load men with burdens that are very hard to be carried. You yourselves will not touch the burdens with one of your fingers. Woe to you! For you build the graves of the prophets, and your fathers killed them. You surely show that you think well of the deeds of your fathers. For they indeed killed the prophets, and you build their graves. Because of this God said that He

206

would send prophets and apostles. Some of them you will kill and harm. You will be guilty of all the blood of all the prophets who were killed. Woe to you, lawyers! For you have taken away the key of knowledge. You did not enter in yourselves, and you hindered those who were entering in."

As Jesus said these things to the lawyers, the scribes and Pharisees began to strongly urge Him to talk about many things. They were watching for Him to say something for which they could accuse Him.

Lesson 17

Jesus Teaches His Disciples

Luke 12:1–13:9

As Jesus was talking to the hypocrites, so many people gathered together that they could not be counted. They were crowded so thickly that they trampled on each other.

Jesus said to His disciples, "Beware of the teaching of the Pharisees. It is hypocrisy." The Pharisees tried to hide their sins and appear righteous. But Jesus said, "There is nothing covered that shall not be seen. There is nothing hid that shall not be known." Someday all hidden sin will be clearly seen.

Jesus knew that He would be killed by wicked men. He knew also that wicked men would seek to kill His followers. He said to His disciples, "My friends, do not be afraid of those who kill the body and after that can do nothing more. I will warn you ahead of time whom you shall fear. Fear Him who, after He has killed, has power to cast into hell. Yes, I say to you, fear Him."

Jesus asked His disciples, "Are not five

sparrows sold for two farthings? Yet even one sparrow is not forgotten by God. But even the very hairs of your head are all numbered. Do not be afraid then. You are of more value than many sparrows.

"Also, I say to you, whoever will confess Me before men, him shall I confess before the angels of God. But he that denies Me before men shall be denied before the angels of God. And whoever speaks against the Son of Man shall be forgiven. But whoever speaks disrespectfully against the Holy Ghost, it shall not be forgiven.

"When men bring you to the synagogues and to rulers, do not be thinking about what you will say. The Holy Ghost will teach you at that same time what you shall say."

One man in the crowd of people said to Jesus, "Master, speak to my brother so that he will divide the inheritance with me."

Jesus said, "Man, who made Me a judge or a divider over you?" Jesus had much more important work to do than to help this man to get some money. It was wrong for this man to be so concerned about getting his share of the money. Jesus said to the people, "Give careful attention, and beware of covetousness, because a man's life is not made up of the things that he owns."

Jesus then told a story to show how foolish it is to want money and the things that money can buy. He told the story also to show how important it is to lay up treasure in heaven. He said, "The ground of a certain rich man grew good crops. The man thought, 'What shall I do? I have no more room to store my crops. This is what I will do. I will pull down my barns and build bigger barns. There I will put all my crops and my goods. I will say to my soul, "Soul, you have a large store of goods laid up for many years. Take it easy. Eat, drink, and be merry." '

"But God had something to say. God said to him, 'You fool, this night your soul shall be required of you. Then whose shall those things be which you have provided for yourself?' "

This is how it is with people who lay up treasures for themselves and do not lay up treasures in heaven. They are rich in this life, but they are not rich toward God. This life is soon over, and then they have nothing.

Jesus said to His disciples, "Do not think about what you will have to eat or what you have to wear. Life is more than food, and the body is more than clothing. Think about the ravens. They do not sow crops or gather them in. They do not have a storehouse or a barn, and yet God feeds them. Of how much greater value are you than the birds?

"Which of you by wishing you were taller can add anything to your stature? If then you are not able to do that which is the smallest thing to do, why do you even think about the rest?

"Think about the lilies, how they grow. They do not work. They do not spin to make clothing. Yet I say to you that Solomon in all his glory was not clothed so wonderfully as the lily. If God is so careful to give a lily a beautiful dress, which lasts for only a short time, will He not also clothe you? Do not be so concerned about what you will eat and what you will drink. Do not have a doubtful mind. The people of this world are interested in these things. They think about them a lot. But you have a Father who knows that you need these things. Seek first the kingdom of God, and these other things will then be supplied. Do not be afraid, little flock, because it is your Father's good pleasure to give you the kingdom.

"Sell what you have and give to the poor. Provide yourselves with bags that do not get old, a treasure in the heavens. This treasure never ends. No thief can steal it there. No moth can eat it. Where your treasure is, there will your heart be also. Keep your minds on the things of God, and let your lights keep shining. Be like men who wait for their lord when he comes back from the wedding so that when he comes and knocks they may open to him immediately.

"Blessed are those servants whom the Lord, when He comes, will find watching. Truly I say to you that He shall gird Himself and make them to sit down to food. And He will come forth and serve them."

At this time some people told Jesus about some Galileans whom Pilate had killed. He had mixed their blood with the sacrifices that the people had made when they worshiped.

Jesus asked them, "Do you think that these Galileans were worse sinners than the other Galileans because this happened to them? I tell you, no; but unless you repent, all of you shall perish in the same way."

Jesus then told them a story. He said, "A certain man had a fig tree planted in his vineyard. He came and looked for fruit on the fig tree, but did not find any. He said to the one who took care of his vineyard, 'See, for three years I came looking for fruit on this fig tree, and find none. Cut it down. Why should we let it burden the ground?'

"The man answered, 'Lord, let it alone this year yet. I will dig around it and put fertilizer around it. If it bears fruit, well. But if not, after that you shall cut it down.' "

This story helps to show that God has much patience with people before He gives them up. Like the Galileans who were not killed, sinners are not always killed right away. God does not want to cut them off from everlasting life. He looks for fruit. The fruit is works that please God. He does much to help people to bear fruit. But if they still will not do His will, He must finally destroy them.

Jesus Heals, Warns, and Teaches
Luke 13:10–14:15

Jesus was teaching in one of the synagogues on the Sabbath Day. A poor woman who was bent over was there. She could not in any way lift herself and stand straight. She had been like this for eighteen years.

When Jesus saw her, He called her. He said, "Woman, you are set free from your infirmity." Jesus laid His hands on her, and immediately she was made straight. She glorified God.

But the ruler of the synagogue was angry. He did not like that Jesus had done this on the Sabbath Day. He said to the people, "There are six days in which men ought to work. In those days come and be healed, and not on the Sabbath Day."

Jesus said to the angry ruler, "You hypocrite, does not each one of you on the Sabbath loose his ox or his ass from the stall and lead him away to give him water? Since this woman is the daughter of Abraham, ought not she, whom Satan has

214

bound these eighteen years, be set free from this bond on the Sabbath Day?"

Jesus' enemies were ashamed when they heard these things. But all the people were happy because of the wonderful things that Jesus did.

Jesus traveled on through the cities and the villages teaching. All the while He was going toward Jerusalem.

Someone asked Him, "Lord, are there few who will be saved?"

Jesus answered, "You must work hard to enter in at the narrow gate because many will seek to enter in and shall not be able. After the door is shut, many will stand outside and knock. They will say, 'Lord, Lord, open to us.'

"The Lord will say, 'I tell you, I do not know from where you are. Depart from Me, all you workers of sin.' There will be weeping and gnashing of teeth when they see Abraham, Isaac, and Jacob and all the prophets in the kingdom of God and themselves cast out. People will come from the east, from the west, from the north, and from the south and shall sit down in the kingdom of God."

The same day that Jesus was teaching these things, some of the Pharisees came to Him. They said, "Get out, and leave here, because Herod will kill You."

Jesus said to them, "Go and tell that fox, 'Behold, I cast out devils and I do cures today and tomorrow. And the third day, I shall be perfected.' Yet, in spite of this, I must walk today and tomorrow and the day following; for it cannot be that a prophet die outside of Jerusalem. O Jerusalem, Jerusalem, you who kill the prophets and stone those who are sent to you. How often would I have gathered your children together, as a hen gathers her brood under her wings, and you would not let Me! Behold, your house is left to you empty. Verily I say to you, you shall not see Me until the time comes when you shall say, 'Blessed is He who comes in the Name of the Lord.' "

Jesus was feeling sad when He said these words. He had come to save these people from their sins, but they would not let Him. Instead, they were going to kill Him at Jerusalem. Even knowing this, He still loved them.

As Jesus went into the house of one of the chief Pharisees to eat bread on the Sabbath Day, they watched Him. A certain man was there who had a disease called dropsy. Jesus asked the

216

lawyers and Pharisees, "Is it right to heal on the Sabbath Day?"

They would not answer Jesus. Jesus took the man and healed him and let him go. He said to the men, "Which of you shall have an ass or an ox that has fallen into a pit and will not immediately pull him out on the Sabbath Day?"

They could not answer Jesus on these things. They were more kind to animals than to people, who have precious souls. This did not make good sense.

Jesus noticed that the people who had come sat in the places of highest honor. Jesus said, "When you are invited to a wedding, do not sit in the highest place, because a more honorable man than you might have been invited. The man who invited the people might say to you, 'Go to a lower place to make room for the more honorable man.' Then you will with shame go down to the lower place. When you are invited, go and sit in the lowest place. Then the one who invites you may say to you, 'Friend, go up higher.' You will then have honor with those with whom you eat. Everyone who tries to make himself great will be put down. Those who humble themselves will be raised to a higher place."

Jesus then spoke to the one who had invited Him to dinner. He said, "When you make a dinner or a supper, do not call your friends or your brothers or your relatives or your rich neighbors, lest they also invite you again, and you are repaid. But when you make a feast, call the poor, the crippled, the lame, and the blind. You will be blessed because they cannot repay you. You will be rewarded at the resurrection of the just."

When one of them who sat eating heard these things, he said to Jesus, "Blessed is he who shall eat bread in the kingdom of God."

Lesson 19

Forgiveness and Salvation

Bring Joy

Luke 14:16–15:32

Jesus told a story to the man who said, "Blessed is he who shall eat bread in the kingdom of God." He said, "A certain man made a great supper. He invited many people. At supper time he sent his servant to tell those who were invited, 'Come, for everything is ready now.'

"But they were called at a time that did not suit them. They had other things that they wanted to do. So they all began to make excuses. The first one said, 'I have bought a piece of ground. I must go and see it. Please have me excused.' Another one said, 'I have bought five yoke of oxen, and I am going to test them. Please have me excused.' Another said, 'I have married a wife; and therefore I cannot come.'

"The servant came back to his master. He told him what the people said. The master was very angry. He had prepared a good meal for these people. Now they would not come. He said to the servant, 'Go out quickly into the streets and lanes of the city, and bring in the poor and the crippled and the lame and the blind.'

"The servant did as he was commanded. Then he said, 'Lord, it is done as you have commanded, and still there is room for more.'

"The master said, 'Go out into the highways and hedges and compel them to come in that my house may be filled. I tell you that none of those men who were invited shall taste of my supper.'"

This story shows how it will be with many people. They will not come to Jesus when He invites them. They will be too interested in the things of this life to leave them to follow Jesus. So they will have many excuses for not coming. Therefore, they will not get to go to heaven to feast on the good things of God there. But the poor, the sick, and the needy will be there because they were ready to come to Jesus when He called. They wanted to come to Him more than anything else.

People must be willing to give up everything for Jesus. They should think about this before they come to Jesus. Then when He asks them to give up their own wishes to serve Him, they will be willing. Jesus said, "Whoever does not forsake all that he has cannot be My disciple." To follow Jesus and have everlasting life is worth giving up everything else.

The publicans and sinners came to Jesus. They loved to listen to Him. The scribes and Pharisees complained about this. They said, "This Man receives sinners and eats with them."

Jesus said to them, "What man of you having a hundred sheep, if he loses one, will not leave the ninety-nine in the wilderness and go after the one which is lost until he finds it? When he has found it, he lays it on his shoulders, rejoicing. When he comes home, he calls together his friends and neighbors. He says to them, 'Rejoice with me, for I have found my sheep that was lost.' I tell you that in the same way there shall be joy in heaven over one sinner who repents more than over ninety-nine just persons who do not need to repent.

"Or what woman having ten pieces of silver, if she loses one piece, will not light a candle and sweep the house and look diligently until she finds it? When she has found it, she calls her friends and her neighbors together. She says, 'Rejoice with me because I have found the piece which I had lost.' In the same way, I tell you, there is joy in the presence of the angels of God over one sinner who repents."

Jesus told yet another story. He said, "A certain man had two sons. The younger son said to his father, 'Father, give me the part of your goods that will become mine.'

"So the father divided his things. He gave to his younger son the things that were to be his.

"Not many days after this, the younger son gathered all his things together. He left home and traveled into a country far away from home. There he wasted the things that he had received from his father. He lived a wild and careless life to please himself.

"When he had spent everything he had, there came a terrible famine in the land. This poor son needed things, and he had no money left to buy anything. So he went to work for a man of that country. This man sent him out to feed the pigs. He was so hungry that he wished he could eat what the pigs ate. But no one gave him even this to eat.

"At last he realized how foolish he had been to run away from home. His father had many hired servants. They had all the food they wanted

222

to eat, and more. Here he was, his father's son, and yet he was dying of hunger!

"He said, 'I will go home. I will say, "Father, I have sinned against heaven and before you. I am no longer worthy to be called your son. Make me as one of your hired servants."'

"He came back to his father. While he was still a long way off, his father saw him. His father ran out to meet him and hugged and kissed him.

"The son said to his father, 'Father, I have sinned against heaven and in your sight. I am no longer worthy to be called your son.'

"The father said to his servants, 'Bring out the best robe and put it on him. Dress him with things to honor him as my son. Bring the calf that was fattened and kill it. Let us eat and be merry, for this my son was dead and is alive again. He was lost and is found.' They began to be merry.

"The father's older son was in the field. As he came near the house, he heard the sounds of rejoicing. He called for one of the servants. He asked, 'What do these things mean?'

"The servant said, 'Your brother has come home. Your father has killed the fat calf because he has received his son safe and sound.'

"When the older brother heard this, he was

angry. He would not go into the house. His father came out and begged him to come in, but the son would not. He said, 'I have worked for you many years. At no time have I disobeyed you. Yet you have never given me a kid so that I could have a good time with my friends. Now as soon as this your son, who has been wasteful and wild, has come home, you have killed for him the fattened calf.'

"The father said, 'Son, you are always with me, and all that I have is yours. It was right that we should make merry and be glad, for your brother was dead and is alive again. He was lost and is found.' "

Lesson 20

The Rich Man and Lazarus

Luke 16

Jesus told His disciples about a certain rich man. He had a steward, who took care of his business. Jesus said, "Some people went to the rich master. They accused the steward of wasting his goods.

"The master called for his steward. He said, 'What is this that I hear about you? Give an account of your stewardship, because you cannot be steward any longer.'

"The steward thought, 'What shall I do? My master is taking my job away from me. I cannot dig. I am ashamed to beg. I know what I will do to gain favor with others, so that they will receive me when my master takes away my job.'

"He called to him all the men who owed money to his master. Beginning with the first one, he asked, 'How much do you owe my master?'

"The debtor said, 'A hundred measures of oil.'

"The steward said, 'Take your bill. Sit down quickly and write fifty.'

225

"The steward said to another debtor, 'And how much do you owe?'

"He answered, 'A hundred measures of wheat.'

"The steward said to him, 'Take your bill and write eighty.' "

Many debtors are never able to pay all they owe. This steward knew how to get them to pay at least some of their debt and to do it quickly. This way the master got more from his debtors than if they never gave anything. Also, the debtors were glad to have the debt gone without having to pay more than they were able to pay. The steward's master praised the man for the wisdom he had shown.

Jesus said to His disciples, "People who are faithful in little things are also faithful in big things. If you are not fair in little things, you will also be unfair in large things. If you are not faithful and honest with your money, God cannot trust you with the true riches of heaven. If you cannot be faithful with another man's money, who will give you your own money?

"No servant can work for two masters. Either he will hate the one and love the other, or else he will hold to the one and despise the other. You cannot serve both God and riches."

The Pharisees heard Jesus say these things. They coveted money. To be rich was their great aim in life. Because of this, they did not like what Jesus said. They made fun of Him because of the things He said.

Jesus said to them, "You are they who try to show yourselves to be good in the eyes of men. But God knows your hearts. That which man thinks very highly of is wickedness in the sight of God."

Jesus told them a story of a rich man who had what money could buy. But he had no treasure in heaven. Jesus said, "There was a certain rich man. He was clothed in very fine clothes. He lived in great luxury every day.

"A certain poor beggar named Lazarus, who was full of sores, was laid at the rich man's gate. He wanted to be fed with the crumbs that fell from the rich man's table. Dogs came and licked his sores.

"At last the poor beggar died. The angels carried him to Abraham. The rich man also died and was buried. He was in hell and in great torments. He looked up and saw Abraham far away. He saw Lazarus in Abraham's bosom.

"The rich man cried out, 'Father Abraham, have mercy on me. Send Lazarus that he may dip the tip of his finger in water and cool my tongue; for I am tormented in this flame.'

"But Abraham said, 'Son, remember that you in your lifetime received your good things. Likewise Lazarus received evil things. But now he is comforted, and you are tormented. And, beside all this, between us and you there is a great gulf fixed so that those who would go from here to you cannot. Neither can any come to us from where you are.'

"Then the man in hell said, 'I pray you, for this reason then, Father, that you would send Lazarus to my father's house. I have five brothers. Have him talk to them lest they also come to this place of torment.'

"Abraham said to him, 'They have Moses and the prophets. Let them listen to them.'

"The man in hell answered, 'No, Father Abraham; but if one goes to them from the dead, they will repent.'

"Abraham answered, 'If they do not listen to Moses and the prophets, neither will they be persuaded though one rose from the dead.'"

Lesson 21

Jesus Teaches Great Lessons
Luke 17

Jesus said to His disciples, "It cannot be helped. Things will happen that offend people. But woe to him who causes another person to sin. It would be better for him to have a millstone hanged about his neck and be thrown into the sea than that he should cause one of these little ones to sin."

Jesus' followers need to be careful to do all that Jesus commands so that they do not cause another person to sin. They need to be just as careful not to let others offend them. So Jesus said, "Be careful about yourselves. If your brother sins against you, rebuke him. If he repents, forgive him. If he sins against you seven times in a day and turns again to you saying, 'I repent,' forgive him."

The twelve apostles knew that this would not be easy to do. To keep on being kind to someone who keeps doing wrong to you does not seem right to men. Yet, because Jesus said to do it, the

229

apostles knew it is right. They felt a need for more faith to believe what Jesus said so that they could obey Him. They said to the Lord, "Increase our faith."

Jesus said, "If you had faith as a grain of mustard seed, you could say to this sycamine tree, 'Be plucked up by the root and be planted in the sea,' and it would obey you." A mustard seed is very small. Jesus was teaching that one does not need a large amount of faith to obey Him.

Jesus knew the hearts of His disciples. He knew that if they forgave their brother often, they might think that the Lord would surely thank them for this. So He asked them, "Which of you, having a servant plowing or feeding cattle, will say to him when he comes from the field, 'Go and sit down to eat'? Will you not rather say, 'Get ready so that I can eat, and serve me until I have finished eating. Afterward, you shall eat and drink'? Does he thank the servant because he did the things that he told him to do? I believe that he will not. So also you, when you have done all the things that you were commanded to do, say, 'We are unprofitable servants. We have done that which was our duty to do.' "

Truly, we are God' servants. It is our duty to

do all that God commands us. God does not owe us thanks for it. What He does for us is so much more than anything we can ever do for Him.

As Jesus entered into a certain village, ten men who were lepers met Him. They stood afar off and cried, "Jesus, Master, have mercy on us."

When Jesus saw them, He said to them, "Go, show yourselves to the priests." As the lepers were on their way to the priests, they were healed.

One of them, when he saw that he was healed, turned back. With a loud voice he glorified God. He fell down on his face before the feet of Jesus and thanked Him.

This thankful man was a Samaritan. The Jews thought they were better than the Samaritans. Yet it was only this Samaritan that came back to thank Jesus.

Jesus said to him, "Were there not ten lepers cleansed? But where are the nine? Is this stranger the only one who has returned to give glory to God?" Jesus said, "Arise. Go your way. Your faith has made you whole."

The Pharisees asked Jesus, "When will the kingdom of God come?"

Jesus said, "The kingdom of God does not come by outward evidence. Do not say, 'Look

231

here,' or 'Look there,' because the kingdom of God is within you. The days will come when you will desire to see Me. But when people say to you, 'See here,' or 'See there,' do not go after them or follow them. My coming will be as the lightning shining from one part of heaven to the other." When Jesus comes, everyone will know it. No one will need to tell others where to find Him.

Jesus told the disciples how it will be on earth when He comes again. First He compared it to the time of Noah. He said, "As it was in the days of Noah, so shall it be also in the days of the Son of Man. They ate and drank. They married wives and were given in marriage until the day that Noah went into the ark and the Flood came and destroyed them all. It was like this also in the days of Lot. People were eating and drinking. They were buying and selling. They were planting and building until the day that Lot went out of Sodom and fire and brimstone rained from heaven and destroyed them all. This is how it will be when the Lord comes again.

"In that day, whoever is on the top of the house and has his things in the house, let him not come down to take them away. And he who is in the field, let him not turn back. Remember Lot's wife. Whoever tries to save his life shall lose it. And whoever shall lose his life shall keep it."

The people in Noah's time were interested in staying alive and having a good time. They did not realize that soon they would be destroyed. Noah knew destruction was coming. He was preparing for that time and escaped drowning in the Flood. Likewise Lot and his wife escaped from Sodom and were not destroyed with the people in it. But after they escaped, Lot's wife disobeyed God's command not to look back. She looked back and died because of it. These examples are a warning to the people of God to prepare for the time when the world will be destroyed with fire.

Jesus said, "I tell you, in that night there shall be two men in one bed. The one shall be taken, and the other left. Two women shall be grinding together. The one shall be taken, and the other left. Two men will be in the field. The one shall be taken, and the other left."

The disciples asked, "Where, Lord?"

Jesus answered, "Wherever the body is, there will the eagles be gathered together."

Lesson 22

Whom Can Jesus Help?

Luke 18

Jesus told His disciples a story. It was to teach them that men should always pray and not grow tired and give up in the Christian life. It would be very sad not to be ready when Jesus comes again. Jesus said, "In a city was a judge who did not fear God or care about the needs of people. A certain widow was in that city. She came to the judge and asked him to punish her enemy.

"For a while the judge would not help her. Still she kept coming to him. He thought, 'Though I do not fear God or care about men, yet because this widow troubles me, I will help her, lest she make me tired by her continual coming.'"

Jesus said, "Listen to what the unjust judge says. If an unjust man will help a widow because she keeps coming to him, how much more will God help His people who come and call upon Him day and night? He may not answer right away, but the punishment of the wicked is sure, and it will

234

happen speedily. However, when the Son of Man comes, will He find faith on the earth?''

With Jesus there were certain people who trusted in themselves. They thought they were righteous, and despised other people.

Jesus said to them, "Two men went into the temple to pray. One of them was a Pharisee. The other was a publican. The Pharisee stood up to pray. He said to himself, 'God, I thank You that I am not as other men are. They are people who charge too much money, unfair people, and adulterers. I thank You that I am not even as this publican. I fast twice in the week. I give tithes of all that I possess.'

"The publican was standing a long way off. He was so ashamed that he would not even lift his eyes to heaven. He hit his chest and said, 'God be merciful to me a sinner.'

"I tell you that this man went down to his house justified rather than the other man. For everyone that brags about himself will be put down, and he that humbles himself shall be lifted up."

The publican was humble. He confessed with sorrow that he was a sinner. Because of this, God could lift him up to become His child. All people

235

who humble themselves before God will receive this same mercy and kindness from Him.

The Pharisee was proud. He did not humble himself and confess with sorrow that he was a sinner. Because of this, God could not lift him up. All people who think they are good and expect to get to heaven because of the good things they do will be disappointed.

Some babies were brought to Jesus so that He would touch them. When the disciples saw it, they rebuked the ones who brought them.

But Jesus said, "Allow little children to come to Me. Do not tell them not to come, for of such is the kingdom of God. Whoever will not receive the kingdom of God as a little child shall not in any way enter into heaven."

A certain ruler asked Jesus, "Good Master, what shall I do to inherit eternal life?"

Jesus said to him, "Why do you call Me good? God is the only One who is good. You know the commandments. Do not commit adultery. Do not kill. Do not steal. Do not tell lies. Honor your father and your mother."

The man answered, "All these things have I kept from my youth up."

When Jesus heard this, He said to him, "You

lack one thing. Sell all that you have, and give it to the poor, and you shall have treasure in heaven. Then come and follow Me."

When the ruler heard this, he was very sorrowful, because he was very rich. He did not want to give up his riches.

When Jesus saw this, He said, "How unlikely it is that those who have riches will enter into the kingdom of God! It is easier for a camel to go through a needle's eye than for a rich man to enter into the kingdom of God."

The people who heard this said, "Who then can be saved?"

Jesus answered, "The things which are impossible with men are possible with God."

Peter said, "Lo, we have left all and followed You."

Jesus said, "There is no one who leaves house, or parents, or brothers, or wife, or children for the kingdom of God's sake who shall not receive much more in this present time. And in the world to come he shall receive life that never ends."

Then Jesus took to Himself the twelve apostles and said, "Behold, we go up to Jerusalem. All things that the prophets have said would happen to the Son of man will come true.

He will be delivered to sinful men. He will be mocked and spit upon. He will be treated very spitefully. He will be whipped and put to death. But on the third day He will rise again.''

Jesus was telling His disciples what was soon going to happen to Him. But they did not understand what Jesus was telling them. The things He said were hidden from them.

As Jesus came near Jericho, a certain blind man sat begging by the side of the road. He could hear that a great multitude was passing by.

''What does this mean?'' the blind man asked.

They answered, ''Jesus of Nazareth is passing by.''

The blind man called to Jesus. He said, ''Jesus, Son of David, have mercy on me.''

The people who were ahead of Jesus rebuked the blind man. They said to him, ''Be quiet.''

But he cried out all the more, ''Son of David, have mercy on me.''

Jesus heard his cry for help. He commanded the blind man to be brought to Him. When he came near, Jesus asked him, ''What do you want Me to do for you?''

He said, ''Lord, that I may receive my sight.''

Jesus said to him, ''Receive your sight. Your

faith has saved you."

Immediately the man received his sight and followed Jesus, glorifying God. When all the people saw it, they praised God.

Zacchaeus and the Nobleman

Luke 19:1-27

After Jesus healed the blind man, He passed through the town of Jericho. A rich man named Zacchaeus lived there. Zacchaeus was a chief among the publicans. He wanted to see Jesus and learn who He was. But because he was very short and many people crowded around Jesus, he could not see Him.

Nevertheless, Zacchaeus was determined to see Him. He ran ahead of the crowd of people. Then he climbed up into a sycamore tree so that he could see Jesus when He passed by.

When Jesus came to the place where Zacchaeus was, He looked up and saw him in the tree. He said to him, "Hurry and come down because I must stay at your house today."

How pleased Zacchaeus was! This was better than he had expected. Not only did he get to see Jesus, but Jesus had spoken to him and was coming to his house! Zacchaeus quickly came down from the tree. He joyfully received Jesus

into his house.

The other people complained about this. They said, "Jesus has gone to be the guest of a man who is a sinner."

Yes, Zacchaeus was a sinner. He was a leader of the despised publicans—men who collected tax money. And they were known for getting rich by taking more money from the people than they were supposed to take.

But Zacchaeus was sorry for his sins. He was ready to make all his wrongs right. He stood and said to the Lord, "Behold, Lord, the half of my goods I give to the poor. And if I have taken anything wrongly from anyone, I will give back to him four times as much as I have taken."

Jesus knew that Zacchaeus meant what he said. Jesus said, "This day salvation has come to this house, because he also is the son of Abraham. For the Son of Man is come to seek and to save that which was lost."

Zacchaeus had looked for Jesus, and Jesus had looked for him. Zacchaeus had gladly received the One who had come to seek and to save the lost. He was ready to do what was right and to be faithful. Therefore, he was the son of Abraham, because Abraham is the father of the faithful.

Everyone who is faithful to the Lord is a child of Abraham as Zacchaeus was.

Jesus was nearing Jerusalem, the capital city. Some people were looking for the kingdom of God to appear there. They thought that Jesus would set up His kingdom on earth and be the king. So Jesus told them this parable:

"A certain nobleman went into a far country to receive a kingdom for himself and then return. He called his ten servants to him. He gave each of them the same amount of money. Each received one pound. He told them to use it to earn more money for him until he returned.

"But the people of his country hated him. They said, 'We will not have this man reign over us.'

"At last the nobleman returned, having received his kingdom. He commanded his servants to whom he had given the money to be called. He wanted them to tell what they had done with their money and how much more money they had gained.

"The first one came and said, 'Lord, your pound has gained ten pounds.'

"The nobleman said, 'Well, you good servant. Because you have been faithful in a very little, have the rule over ten cities.'

"The second servant came. He said, 'Lord, your pound has gained five pounds.'

"The nobleman said to him in the same way as he had said to the first, 'Be ruler over five cities.'

"Another one came. He said, 'Lord, behold, here is your pound which I have kept laid up in a napkin because I was afraid of you. I knew that you are a stern man. You take what you did not give and harvest where you did not sow.'

"The master said to him, 'Out of your own mouth will I judge you, you wicked servant. You knew that I was a stern man, taking up what I did not lay down and harvesting where I did not sow. Because of this, why did you not give my money to the bank so that when I came back I could have gotten back my money with some interest?'

"Then the master commanded, 'Take the pound from him. Give it to the man who has ten pounds. For I tell you, whoever has, to him shall be given. And from him that does not have anything, even what he has shall be taken from him. But those of my enemies who did not want me to reign over them, bring them here and kill

244

them before me.' "

Jesus, like the nobleman, went away to receive a kingdom for Himself. He has given men gifts to use and make increase for Him. Some people hate Him and will not let Him rule over them. They do not make good use of the things He gave them. But anyone who makes good use of the things He has given to them so that they have something to give back to Him, God will reward. If they do not gain anything for Him, even what He gave them will be taken away from them.

Lesson 24

Jesus at Jerusalem

Luke 19:28–20:18

Near Jerusalem, on the Mount of Olives, were two small towns, Bethphage and Bethany. When Jesus came close to one of these villages, He said to two of His disciples, "Go into the village. When you enter, you will find a colt tied on which no one ever sat yet. Loose him and bring him here. If anyone asks you, 'Why do you loose him?' say to him, 'Because the Lord needs him.'"

The two disciples went and found the colt just as the Lord had said. As they were untying him, the owners of the colt asked, "Why do you loose the colt?"

They answered, "The Lord needs him."

Then they brought the colt to Jesus. They put some of their clothes on the colt and put Jesus on it. As Jesus rode on the colt, the people put down their clothes in the path ahead.

When Jesus came near the foot of the Mount of Olives, the whole multitude of the disciples began to rejoice. They praised God with a loud voice because of all the mighty works that they had seen. They said, "Blessed be the King who comes in the Name of the Lord. Peace in heaven, and glory in the highest."

The Pharisees did not like to hear this praise. Some of them said to Jesus, "Master, rebuke Your disciples."

But Jesus said, "If they would keep still, the stones would immediately cry out."

When Jesus came near to Jerusalem, He looked at the city and wept over it. He said, "If you had known, even you, at least in this your day, the things which are to your peace! But now they are hid from your eyes. For the days shall come upon you that your enemies shall build a ditch around you. They will surround the city and keep you in on every side. They shall lay you and your children even with the ground. They shall not leave one stone upon another because you did not know the time when you were visited."

Jesus said these things because He knew that Jerusalem was going to be destroyed. He longed that the people would understand their need of Him, and come to Him before it was too late. Jesus loves to have mercy on people. He wept because they would not come to Him for mercy and would have to receive great punishment.

At Jerusalem, Jesus went into the temple. There He saw something that made Him very sad. People were buying and selling in the temple. Jesus made them get out. He said, "It is written, 'My house is the house of prayer.' But you have made it a den of thieves."

Each day Jesus taught in the temple. The chief priests and the scribes and the chief of the people kept watching for a way to destroy Him. They did not know how to do it because the people were eager to hear Him.

Jesus continued to teach the people and to preach the Gospel in the temple. The chief priests, the scribes, and the elders came to Him. They asked, "By what authority do You do these things? Who gave You this right?"

Jesus said to them, "I will also ask you one thing. Answer Me. Was the baptism of John from heaven or of men?"

The men thought about this question and talked among themselves. They did not know how to answer Jesus. They said, "If we say that John's baptism was from heaven, Jesus will say, 'Then why did you not believe him?' If we say, 'Of men,' all the people will stone us because they are

248

persuaded that John was a prophet.' They wanted to trap Jesus in His answers, but they did not want to be trapped by their own answers. So they said to Jesus, "We cannot tell from where John's baptism was."

Jesus had a good answer for this, too. He said to them, "Neither do I tell you by what authority I do these things." This was only fair. They should not expect an answer if they were not willing to answer Jesus.

Jesus taught the people with a parable. He said, "A certain man planted a vineyard. He rented the vineyard to farmers and went into a far country. He intended that the farmers should give him some of the fruit of the vineyard.

"At the right season, when the grapes were ripe, he sent a servant to the farmers to get some of the fruit for him. The farmers beat the servant and sent him away empty.

"Then the owner of the vineyard sent another servant. They also beat this servant and treated him shamefully. They sent him away without any fruit.

"The owner sent a third servant. But the farmers wounded him and threw him out of the vineyard.

"The owner of the vineyard said, 'What shall I do? I will send my beloved son. It may be that they will respect him when they see him.'

"But when the wicked farmers saw the son, they said, 'This is the one who will get the vineyard when his father dies. Come, let us kill him, that the vineyard may be ours.' So they threw him out of the vineyard and killed him.

"Because of this, what will the owner of the vineyard do to them? He will come and destroy these farmers and shall give the vineyard to others."

When the people heard this, they said, "God forbid."

Jesus looked at them and said, "What is this then that is written, 'The stone which the builders rejected, the same is become the head of the corner'? Whosoever shall fall upon that stone shall be broken. But on whomsoever it shall fall, it will grind him to powder."

The story that Jesus told shows us what the Jews had done. They had killed God's servants, the prophets, whom God had sent to them. At last God sent His well-beloved and only Son, Jesus. Now they were planning to kill Him also, and He knew that they would kill Him. He is the chief

250

cornerstone in God's holy temple. Those who come to Him will be brokenhearted. They will be sorry for their sins and serve Him because they love Him. But those who do not come to Him and are not brokenhearted will sometime have God's Son fall on them in fearful judgment.

Lesson 25

Jesus Answers Jewish Leaders

Luke 20:19–21:38

The chief priests and the scribes understood that the story Jesus told was against them. They wanted to get rid of Jesus, but they were afraid of the people. The people loved Jesus. If they killed Jesus, the people would not praise them, and they loved men's praise.

They kept watching Jesus. They even sent spies who would pretend to be good men. They were to catch Jesus in His words so that He could be accused of sin. Then the chief priests and scribes would deliver Him to the governor, who would have power to condemn Him to death. The Roman law did not allow the Jews to sentence a man to death and kill him.

The spies said to Jesus, "Master, we know that You speak and teach rightly. You teach the way of God truly. Is it right for us to pay tax to Caesar, or not?"

Jesus knew that these men were hypocrites and only pretending that they really wanted to

252

know what was right. He knew they were trying to catch Him in His words. He said, "Why do you tempt Me? Show Me a penny. Whose picture and name is on it?"

They answered, "Caesar's."

Jesus said to them, "Because of this, give to Caesar the things that are Caesar's, and to God the things that are God's."

The men could not find fault with these words. They marveled at His answer and kept still.

The Sadducees said that there is no resurrection. They did not believe that the righteous go to heaven when they die. They thought they always stay dead. Some of them came to Jesus. They said, "Master, Moses wrote us that if a man dies and has no children, his brother should take his wife and raise children for his brother. There were seven brothers. The first took a wife and died without having any children. The second brother took her for his wife. He also died without any children. The third took her and had no children. In the same way, all seven had her for a wife and died without children. Last of all, the woman died also. In the resurrection, whose wife is she because all seven of them had her as a wife?"

Jesus said to them, "In this life people marry

and are given in marriage. But those who are counted worthy to go to heaven and rise from the dead do not marry, and they cannot die any more. They are equal to the angels and are the children of God, being children of the resurrection. That the dead are raised, even Moses showed at the bush when he called the Lord the God of Abraham, and the God of Isaac, and the God of Jacob. For God is not a God of the dead, but of the living, for all live to Him.''

The scribes believed in a resurrection, and they liked Jesus' answer to the Sadducees. Some of them said, ''Master, You have spoken well.'' After this no one dared to ask Jesus any questions.

In the audience of all the people Jesus spoke to His disciples. He said, ''Beware of the scribes. They desire to walk in long robes. They love greetings in the markets and the highest seats in the synagogues and the chief places at feasts. They devour widows' houses, and for a show make long prayers. They shall receive greater damnation.''

Jesus looked up and saw the rich men throwing their gifts into the treasury. He also saw a certain poor widow throwing in two small coins.

254

Jesus said, "Truly I say to you that this poor widow has thrown in more than all of them." He said this because the rich had thrown in of their abundance of money. It was really very little in comparison to the great amount of money they had. But the poor widow had thrown in all that she had.

Some were talking together about the temple. They admired the costly and beautiful stones and gifts that adorned it. Jesus said, "As for these things which you see, the days will come when there shall not be left one stone upon another that shall not be thrown down."

The people asked Him, "Master, but when will this happen? What signs will there be that it will be destroyed?"

Jesus then told them some of the things that would happen before Jerusalem would be destroyed. He also told them things that would happen before He comes again.

He said, "Be careful that you are not deceived. Many shall come in My Name. They will say, 'I am Christ.' Do not go after them. When you hear of wars and commotion do not be terrified. These things must first happen, but the end is not yet. Nation shall rise against nation. Kingdom shall rise against kingdom. Great earthquakes will be in different places. There will be famines, diseases, and fearful sights and great signs from heaven.

"But before all these things, they shall lay hands on you and persecute you. They will put you into prisons. You will be brought before kings and rulers for My Name's sake. This will be your chance to testify for Me.

"Because of this, settle it in your hearts not to think beforehand what you will say to them. I will give you a mouth and wisdom which all your enemies will not be able to speak against or resist. When these things begin to happen, look up and lift up your heads, for your redemption draws near.

"Look at the fig tree and all trees. When they bud, you see and know that summer is now near. So, in the same way, when you see these things happen, know that the kingdom of God is near. Truly I say to you, this generation shall not pass away till all things happen that God said would happen. Heaven and earth shall pass away, but My words shall not pass away.

"Watch and pray that you may be able to escape all these things that will happen."

In the daytime Jesus taught in the temple. But at night He stayed in the Mount of Olives. Early in the morning the people gathered at the temple to hear Him again.

The Passover

Luke 22:1-38

Now the time that the Jews keep the feast of the Passover drew near. This feast was to remind them of the time that God brought His people out of their slavery in Egypt. Each family or group of families had killed a lamb. Its blood had been put on the top and on the sides of the door of the house. Then at midnight the Lord had passed through to destroy the first-born in every home where there was no blood on the door. But He had passed over every home where He saw blood on the door. The first-born in that house was spared from being killed. The feast of the Passover was to remind them of this time of deliverance from death and from slavery in Egypt.

The feast of the Passover was also to help God's people to look forward to the time when Jesus, the Lamb of God, would be killed. By shedding His blood, He would deliver His people from the bondage of sin. They would not have to die in their sins if they trusted Jesus' blood to cleanse them from all sin. This feast was sometimes called the Feast of Unleavened Bread. Only unleavened bread was to be eaten for seven days during the feast.

The chief priests and the scribes were still trying to find a way to kill Jesus. But they were afraid of the people. How could they kill Jesus without having all the people turn against them?

Then Satan entered into Judas Iscariot, one of the twelve apostles of Jesus. He went to the chief priests and captains. They talked together about putting Jesus to death. Judas offered to help them by betraying Jesus to them when the people were not around.

The chief priests and captains were very glad for this help from Judas. They agreed to give him money for doing it. That was what Judas wanted. He loved money more than he loved Jesus. He promised to deliver Jesus to them. From that time on, he looked for a chance to betray Jesus to His enemies when the multitude was absent.

Then came the day of unleavened bread when the Passover must be killed. Jesus sent Peter and John to get ready for this feast. He said, "Go, and prepare the Passover for us that we may eat."

"Where do you want us to prepare it?" they

asked.

Jesus said to them, "Behold, when you have entered into the city, a man carrying a pitcher of water shall meet you. Follow him into the house that he enters. Say to the master of that house, 'The Master says to you, "Where is the guest room, where I shall eat the Passover with My disciples?"' He will show you a large upper room. It will be furnished. There get the Passover ready."

Peter and John went as they were told. When they came to the city, they met a man carrying a pitcher of water. They followed him into the house where he went. They said to the master of the house, "The Master says to you, 'Where is the guest room, where I shall eat the Passover with My disciples?'"

The master of the house showed them a large upper room. It was furnished with a table and all that they needed. There they prepared to eat the Passover with Jesus.

When the hour came that they should eat the Passover, Jesus and the twelve apostles sat down together. Jesus said to them, "I have a great desire to eat this Passover with you before I suffer. For I say to you, I will not eat of it any

260

more until it is fulfilled in the kingdom of God."

Then Jesus took the cup. He gave thanks and said, "Take this and divide it among yourselves. For I say to you, I will not drink of the fruit of the vine until the kingdom of God shall come."

Jesus took bread and gave thanks. He broke the bread and gave it to the disciples. He said, "This is My body, which is given for you. This do in remembrance of Me."

After supper He also took the cup. He said, "This cup is the New Testament in My blood, which is shed for you."

Jesus knew that the one who would betray Him was at the table with Him. The Scripture had said that He would be betrayed by one of His friends. Jesus knew that it would be as the Scripture said. Yet it was wrong for Judas to do it. He would suffer for his sin of betraying his Master.

Jesus said, "Behold, the hand of him who betrays Me is with Me on the table. And truly the Son of Man goes as it was determined. But woe to that man by whom He is betrayed!"

The disciples began to inquire among themselves which of them it was that should do this thing. They also argued about which one would be the greatest.

Jesus said to them, "The kings of the Gentiles act as lords over them. But you shall not be like them. He that is greatest among you, let him be as the younger. And he that is chief, as he that serves. For which is greater—he that sits down to eat, or he that serves? Is not he that sits down to eat? But I am among you as He that serves.

"You are they who have continued with Me in My temptations. And I appoint to you a kingdom, as My Father has appointed Me, that you may eat and drink at My table in My kingdom, and sit on thrones, judging the twelve tribes of Israel."

The Lord said, "Simon, Simon, behold, Satan has desired to have you, that he may sift you as wheat. But I have prayed for you so that your faith will not fail. When you are converted, strengthen your brethren."

Peter said to Jesus, "Lord, I am ready to go with You both to prison and to death."

Jesus said to him, "I tell you, Peter, the rooster shall not crow today before you shall deny three times that you know Me."

Jesus asked the disciples, "When I sent you without purse and shoes, did you lack anything?"

They answered, "Nothing."

Jesus said to them, "But now he who has a purse, let him take it. And he who has no sword, let him sell his garment and buy one."

They said, "Lord, look! Here are two swords."

Jesus said to them, "It is enough."

Jesus in Gethsemane

Luke 22:39-71

Jesus went, as He often did, to the Mount of Olives. His disciples followed Him. He said to them, "Pray that you do not enter into temptation."

Jesus went a short distance away from them—about as far as a person can throw a stone. There He kneeled down and prayed. He said, "Father, if You are willing, remove this cup from Me. Yet not My will, but Yours be done."

An angel from heaven appeared to Jesus and gave Him strength. Jesus was in agony and prayed more earnestly. Great drops of sweat like blood fell down from His body to the ground.

When Jesus arose from prayer, He came to His disciples. He found them sleeping because of their sorrow. He said to them, "Why do you sleep? Get up and pray, lest you enter into temptation."

While Jesus was still speaking, a multitude of people came, with Judas leading the way. Judas chose this time because the people were not with

Jesus. It was night, and Jesus was alone with His disciples on the Mount of Olives.

Judas came near to Jesus to kiss Him.

Jesus asked, "Judas, do you betray the Son of Man with a kiss?"

The disciples who were near Jesus saw what was going to happen. They asked, "Lord, shall we kill with the sword?" Peter took his sword and cut off the ear of Malchus, the servant of the high priest.

Jesus said to Peter, "Put your sword back into its place, for all who take the sword shall die with the sword." Jesus did not want His followers to kill His enemies. He loved them and had come to die for them that they might be saved. Jesus touched and healed the ear of Malchus.

Jesus then spoke to the chief priests, the captains of the temple, and the elders who had come out to Him. He said, "Have you come out as against a thief with swords and staves? I sat daily with you in the temple. You did not put out your hands against Me. But this is your hour and the power of darkness."

Before this it was not God's time for Jesus to die. Therefore, no one could harm Him. Now it was God's time for Jesus to die. God was going to let His enemies crucify His Son. Jesus had been telling His disciples that this would happen, but they did not understand.

The Jews then took Jesus and led Him to the house of the high priest. Peter followed a long way off. A fire was started in the middle of the hall, and the people sat down together. Peter came also and sat down among them.

A certain maid watched Peter very closely as he sat by the fire. She recognized him as one of the men who had been with Jesus. She said, "This man was with Jesus, too."

Peter was afraid and denied that this was true. He said, "Woman, I do not know Him."

After a little while, a man saw Peter. He also recognized him as being one who had been with Jesus. He said to him, "You are of them, too."

Again Peter denied, saying, "Man, I am not."

About one hour after this, another man was sure that Peter had been with Jesus as the others had said. He said, "Truly this fellow also was with Him, for he is a Galilean."

Peter said, "Man, I do not know what you are saying." That very moment, while Peter was still speaking, the rooster crowed.

The Lord turned and looked at Peter. Then

266

Peter remembered that Jesus had said, "Before the rooster crows, you shall deny Me three times."

Peter had done exactly what he had declared he would not do. He had denied Jesus, his very best friend. Peter was sorry for what he had done. He went out and wept bitterly.

The men who had made Jesus a prisoner made fun of Him and hit Him. Then they blindfolded Him and hit Him on the face. They said, "Prophesy. Who hit You?" They also said many other mean things against Him.

As soon as it was daytime, the elders, the chief priests, and the scribes came together. They led Jesus into their council. They asked Him, "Are You the Christ? Tell us."

Jesus said, "If I tell you, you will not believe. If I also ask, you will not answer Me or let Me go. After this the Son of Man shall sit on the right hand of the power of God."

They all asked, "Are You then the Son of God?"

Jesus answered, "You say that I am."

They said, "What need have we of more witness? For we ourselves have heard of His own mouth."

Lesson 28

Jesus Is Tried and Crucified

Luke 23:1-38

All the people rose up and led Jesus to Pilate, the governor. They began to accuse Jesus before Pilate. They said, "Jesus is working against the nation. He says that taxes should not be paid to Caesar. He says that He Himself is Christ the King."

Pilate asked Jesus, "Are You the King of the Jews?"

Jesus answered, "You have said it."

Pilate said to the chief priests, "I do not find any fault in this Man."

When Pilate said this, the people were fiercer than ever. They wanted Jesus killed. They accused Him of causing a stir among the people all the way from Galilee to Jerusalem.

When Pilate heard this, he asked, "Is Jesus a Galilean?" As soon as he knew that Jesus was from Galilee, he sent Him to King Herod because Herod ruled Galilee.

Herod was at Jerusalem at this time. When

he saw Jesus, he was very glad because for a long time he had wanted to see Jesus. He had heard many things about Him, and he hoped to see Him do some miracle. Herod asked Jesus many things, but Jesus would not answer him.

The chief priests and scribes stood up and began to accuse Jesus strongly. Herod and his men of war treated Him very cruelly and sent Him back to Pilate. Up to this time, Pilate and Herod had been enemies. But now, through the trial of Jesus, they became friends.

Pilate called together the chief priests and rulers. He said to them, "You have brought Jesus as a man who leads the people into sin. But I have examined Him before you, and have found no fault with Him about the things of which you accuse Him. No, and Herod has found no fault with Him either. I sent you to Herod and, behold, nothing worthy of death is found in Him. I will therefore whip Him and let Him go."

Now at the feast of the Passover it was necessary for Pilate to set a prisoner free for the Jews. Pilate wanted Jesus to be that prisoner.

But the Jews did not want to hear this. They cried out all at once, saying, "Away with this Man, and release to us Barabbas."

269

Now Barabbas was a real troublemaker. He was a murderer and, because of his wicked deeds, he had been put into prison. The Jews asked that this man go free rather than Jesus, who did no sin.

Pilate spoke to the Jews again because he did not want to condemn Jesus to death.

The Jews cried out, "Crucify Him! Crucify Him!"

Pilate said to them the third time, "Why? What evil has He done? I find no reason that He should be put to death. I will whip Him and let Him go."

Immediately the Jews shouted, demanding that Jesus be crucified. They were so insistent that Pilate gave the word that Jesus should die. He let Barabbas, the murderer, go free and let them do to Jesus as they wished.

Then Jesus was led out to be crucified. On the way they saw a man coming out of the country. They made him carry the cross on which Jesus was to be crucified.

Many people, including women who were friends of Jesus, followed after Him and wept. They were sorry to see their Master mistreated in this way.

Jesus turned to them and said, "Daughters of Jerusalem, do not weep for Me. Weep for yourselves and for your children."

Besides Jesus, two thieves were also led with Him to be put to death. When they came to Calvary, they crucified Jesus, with one thief on one side of Him and the other thief on the other side.

Jesus had no hard feelings toward those who crucified Him. He prayed for them, saying, "Father, forgive them, for they do not know what they do."

His enemies took Jesus' clothes and cast lots to see who should get them.

The people stood watching Jesus. They and the rulers still made fun of Him. They said, "He saved others. Let Him save Himself if He is the Christ, the chosen of God." But they did not understand. Jesus did not come to save Himself. He came to save others, and in order to save sinners, He had to die.

Even the soldiers mocked Jesus. They came to Him, offering Him vinegar to drink. They said, "If You are the King of the Jews, save Yourself."

On the cross above Jesus' head, they put a

writing in three different languages. In Greek, in Hebrew, and in Latin they wrote, "This is the King of the Jews."

Lesson 29

Jesus' Death, Burial,

and Resurrection

Luke 23:39–24:12

One of the two thieves hanging on the cross beside Jesus demanded, "If You are Christ, save Yourself and us."

The other thief knew that he was a sinner and did not deserve to be saved. He rebuked the first thief for speaking as he did. He said, "Do you not fear God, seeing you are in the same condemnation? We deserve to die, but Jesus has done no wrong."

This thief then said to Jesus, "Lord, remember me when You come into Your kingdom."

Jesus said to him, "Truly I say to you, today you shall be with Me in paradise."

From twelve o'clock noon until three o'clock in the afternoon there was darkness over all the earth. The sun was darkened. The veil in the temple was torn in the middle from the top to the

273

bottom. Jesus cried with a loud voice, "Father, into Your hands I commend My spirit." When He said this, He gave up His life.

When the centurion saw what was done, he glorified God. He said, "Certainly this was a righteous Man."

All the people who had come together to that sight hit themselves on the chest and left. All the people who knew Jesus, and the women who had followed Him from Galilee, stood a long way off, watching these things.

There was a just man named Joseph, who was from the Jewish city of Arimathaea. He was a member of the Jewish council. He had not given his permission to have Jesus killed because he believed that Jesus is truly the Son of God. He went to Pilate and begged for the body of Jesus.

With Pilate's permission, Joseph took Jesus' body down from the cross. He wrapped it in linen and put it into a tomb in which no one had yet been buried. This was the day to prepare for the Sabbath Day, and the Sabbath was drawing near.

The women who had followed Jesus from Galilee followed behind Joseph. They saw the tomb and how Jesus was laid in it. Then they left and prepared spices and ointments to anoint the body of Jesus. They rested on the Sabbath Day according to the commandment of the Law of Moses.

On the first day of the week, very early in the morning, they and others with them came to the grave. They brought with them the spices which they had prepared for Jesus' body.

What a surprise they had when they arrived at the grave! They found the stone rolled away— the great stone that had closed the entrance into the tomb. So they went inside, but then they had another surprise. They could not find the body of Jesus. It was not there! This puzzled them greatly. What had happened to His body?

While they were wondering about this, two men in shining clothes stood beside them. The women were frightened and bowed down their faces to the earth. The men said, "Why do you look for the living among the dead? He is not here, but is risen. Remember what He said to you when He was still in Galilee. He said, 'The Son of Man must be delivered into the hands of sinful men and be crucified and, on the third day, rise again.' "

The women then remembered that Jesus had said that. What wondrous comfort! Jesus is not dead. He is alive forevermore!

275

The women went and told the good news to the apostles. But the apostles did not believe them. To them it sounded like a made-up story.

Peter got up and ran to the tomb. He wanted to see for himself. When he came to the grave, he found the linen clothes in which Jesus had been buried. They were lying by themselves. But the body of Jesus was not there. Peter left, wondering about the things that had happened.

Lesson 30

The Ascension

Luke 24:13-53

The same day that Jesus' body could not be found in the grave, two disciples went to a village called Emmaus. It was about seven miles from Jerusalem. As they walked, they were talking about all the things that had just happened. As they talked together and were trying to figure out the puzzling events, Jesus Himself came near. He walked along with them. They did not know that this person walking with them was Jesus. God kept them from knowing Him.

Jesus said to them, "What are these things that you are talking about to one another as you walk and are sad?"

One of them asked, "Are You a stranger at Jerusalem? Do You not know what things are happening there these days?"

"What things?" asked Jesus.

They answered, "Jesus of Nazareth was a prophet mighty in deed and word before God and all the people. And the chief priests and our rulers

277

delivered Him to be put to death and have crucified Him. But we believed that He would be the one to redeem Israel. Besides all this, this is the third day since these things were done. Yes, and certain women also of our group were early at the grave. They astonished us, saying that they could not find His body. They said they had seen angels who said that Jesus is alive. Some of those who were with us went to the grave. They found it just as the women had said, but they did not see Jesus."

Jesus said to them, "O fools and slow of heart to believe all that the prophets have spoken. Ought not Christ to have suffered these things and to enter into His glory?" Then Jesus began to tell them what the Old Testament Scriptures said about Himself. Beginning with the writings of Moses and the prophets, He explained to them in all the Scriptures the things about Himself.

They came near to the village to which they were going. Jesus made it appear as though He intended to go on farther. They said, "Stay with us, for it is toward evening, and the day is almost gone."

Jesus accepted their invitation and went in to stay with them. As He was sitting at the table with them, He took bread and blessed it. He broke the bread and gave it to them. Immediately their eyes were opened. They recognized Jesus. Then He disappeared out of their sight.

They got up from the table that same hour and returned to Jerusalem. There they found the eleven apostles and others together, who said to them, "The Lord is risen indeed and has appeared to Simon!" Then they told what had happened while they were on the way to Emmaus. They also told how they recognized Him while He was breaking bread.

As they were telling their story, Jesus Himself stood among them. He said to them, "Peace be to you."

But they were terrified and frightened. It was a strange thing for someone to suddenly appear in a room without coming in at any door. They thought they had seen a spirit.

Jesus said to them, "Why are you troubled? And why do thoughts arise in your hearts? Look at My hands and My feet, that it is I Myself. Handle Me and see. A spirit does not have flesh and bones as you see that I have." When He had said this, He showed them His hands and His feet.

They were so filled with joy that they still did

not believe.

Jesus said to them, "Have you here any meat?"

The disciples gave Him a piece of broiled fish and a piece of honeycomb. He ate it before them. He said, "These are the words that I spoke to you while I was still with you. I told you that all things must happen which were written in the Law of Moses and in the prophets and in the Psalms about Me."

Jesus caused them to understand the Scriptures. He said, "It was necessary for Christ to suffer and to rise from the dead the third day. Repentance shall be preached in My Name among all nations, beginning at Jerusalem. You are witnesses of these things. And, behold, I send the promise of My Father upon you. But stay in the city of Jerusalem until you receive power from on high."

Jesus led them out as far as Bethany. There He lifted up His hands and blessed them. While He blessed them, He was parted from them and was carried up into heaven. A cloud hid Him from them.

The disciples worshiped Jesus and returned to Jerusalem with great joy. There they were continually in the temple, praising and blessing God.

Pronunciation Symbols
Used in the Glossary

/ā/	as in pay		/a/	as in hat
/ē/	as in see		/e/	as in yes
/ī/	as in by		/i/	as in sit
/ō/	as in go		/o/	as in top
/ū/	as in cube		/u/	as in bug
/ōō/	as in food		/oo/	as in foot

/ou/	as in out		/sh/	as in she
/oi/	as in boy		/ch/	as in chop
/ô/	as in saw		/wh/	as in when
/ä/	as in park		/th/	as in thin
/ė/	as in her		/th/	as in that
/ə/	the indefinite vowel sound heard in an unaccented syllable, representing any of the five vowels, as in *a*lone, list*e*n, flex*i*ble, c*o*nsider, s*u*ppose		/ng/	as in sing
			/zh/	as in measure

Glossary

absent (ab′sənt) *adjective:* Away; not present

acceptable (ak•sep′tə•bəl) *adjective:* Agreeable; good enough

account (ə•kount′) *noun:* A report of what happened

advantage (ad•van′tāj) *noun:* A gain or benefit

affliction (ə•flik′shən) *noun:* Pain, trouble, or distress

agony (ag′ə•nē) *noun:* A very strong feeling of pain or distress

Ahasuerus (ā•haz•ū•ē′rəs) *noun:* A king of Persia who married the Jewish Queen Esther

Alphaeus (al•fē′əs) *noun:* The father of an apostle named James

amen (ā′men′) *interjection:* Agreement; let it be that way

Amos (ā′məs) *noun:* 1. A prophet who lived about the same time as Isaiah and Hosea 2. A book of the Old Testament

apostles (ə•pos′əlz) *noun:* The twelve special disciples Jesus chose to preach the Gospel

appeased (ə•pēzd′) *verb:* Calmed; satisfied

Arimathaea (ar•ə•mə•thē′ä) *noun:* The hometown of the

283

Joseph who buried the body of Jesus

array (ə•rā′) *verb:* Dress up in fine clothes

arrest (ə•rest′) *verb:* To catch and put into prison

Artaxerxes (är•tə•zėrk′sēz) *noun:* A king of Persia in the time of Ezra

ass (as) *noun:* A donkey

attended (ə•tend′əd) *verb:* Went with and took care of

audience (ô′dē•əns) *noun:* 1. Group of people who are hearing 2. The act of hearing; attention

Augustus (ô•gus′təs) *noun:* The Roman ruler at the time Jesus was born

authority (ə•thôr′ə•tē) *noun:* Power to make others obey

babe (bāb) *noun:* Baby

bandaged (ban′dājd) *verb:* Wrapped or covered a wound

banishment (ban′ish•mənt) *noun:* A punishment of forcing someone to stay away from his home or country

banquet (bang′kwet) *noun:* A feast or big dinner

beckoned (bek′ənd) *verb:* Made a sign or signal with the hand

Beelzebub (bē•el′zē•bub) *noun:* The prince of evil spirits

behold (bē•hōld′) *verb:* See; look at

284

Belshazzar (bel•shaz'ər) *noun:* A king of Babylon in Daniel's time

Bethphage (beth'fāj) *noun:* A place on the Mount of Olives near Bethany

betray (bē•trā') *verb:* Be unfaithful; hand over to the enemy

bier (bir) *noun:* A frame on which a dead body is carried

blush (blush) *verb:* To become red because of feeling ashamed or embarrassed

boasted (bōst'əd) *verb:* Spoke proudly of oneself

bond (bond) *noun:* 1. Something that ties or binds 2. A condition that hinders, such as sickness

booths (bōōths) *noun:* Small closed-in places

bosom (booz'əm) *noun:* The upper front part of the human body

bramble (bram'bəl) *noun:* A shrub covered with thorns that prick

brimstone (brim'stōn) *noun:* Sulfur; a substance that burns with a blue flame and creates a strong odor

brow (brou) *noun:* 1. The part of the face above the eyes 2. The top edge of a steep place

Calvary (kal'və•rē) *noun:* A hill near Jerusalem where Jesus was crucified

cankerworm (kang′kər•wərm) *noun:* A caterpillar that eats leaves

Capernaum (kə•pėr′nā•əm) *noun:* A city on the north-west shore of the Sea of Galilee

cargo (kär′gō) *noun:* A load of goods

centurion (sen•toor′ē•ən) *noun:* A Roman officer who had charge of one hundred soldiers

Chaldees (kal′dēz) *noun:* 1. Chaldeans 2. The area or kingdom of Babylon

Chebar (kē′bär) *noun:* A river in the land of the Chaldeans

compel (kom•pel′) *verb:* Urge with force

condemn (kon•dem′) *verb:* To declare a person guilty and worthy of punishment

condemnation (kon•dem•nā′shən) *noun:* The act of condemning or the state of being condemned

converted (kon•vėrt′əd) *verb:* Changed

copper (kop′ər) *noun:* A reddish brown metal

couch (kouch) *noun:* A piece of furniture or a mat on which to sleep or relax

council (koun′səl) *noun:* A group of people who give advice or answer questions

countenance (koun′tə•nəns) *noun:* The face

286

cupbearer (kup′ber•ər) *noun:* One who fills cups and serves drinks

custom (kus′təm) *noun:* The usual way of doing something; habit

Cyrus (sī′rus) *noun:* The Persian king who ruled Babylon after Darius the Median

Darius (də•rī′əs) *noun:* 1. The Median king who had Daniel put into the den of lions 2. The Persian king who helped the Jews to finish building the temple

dealt (delt) *verb:* Acted or behaved

decorations (dek•ə•rā′shənz) *noun:* Things used to make a place beautiful

decree (dē•krē′) 1. *noun:* An order or command 2. *verb:* To order or command

dedication (ded•i•kā′shən) *noun:* The act of setting something apart for a special purpose, such as for the work of the Lord

denied (dē•nīd′) *verb:* Said that something was not true

deny (dē•nī′) *verb:* To declare that something is not true

devour (dē•vour′) *verb:* Eat up or destroy

diligently (dil′ə•jənt•lē) *adverb:* Carefully and steadily

disobedient (dis•ō•bē′dē•ent) *adjective:* Not obeying

distinctly (dis•tingkt′lē) *adverb:* Clearly and plainly

distressing (dis•tres′ing) *adjective:* Causing sorrow, trouble, or pain

dunghill (dung′hil) *noun:* A heap of manure

elders (el′dərz) *noun:* 1. People who are older 2. A group of men in high position among the Jews

Elisabeth (ē•liz′ə•beth) *noun:* The wife of Zacharias and mother of John the Baptist

Emmaus (ē•mā′əs) *noun:* A village about seven and one-half miles from Jerusalem

endures (en•do͞orz′) *verb:* Keeps on

Ephratah (ef′rə•tä) *noun:* An old name for Bethlehem

Esther (es′tər) *noun:* 1. A beautiful Jewess who became the queen of the Persian king Ahasuerus 2. A book of the Old Testament

evidence (ev′ə•dens) *noun:* Proof; something that indicates the truth

Ezekiel (ē•zē′kē•əl) *noun:* 1. A prophet who had unusual visions 2. A book of the Old Testament

Ezra (ez′rä) *noun:* 1. A priest and scribe at the time the Jews returned from the captivity 2. A book of the Old Testament

farthings (fär′<u>th</u>ingz) *noun:* Coins of a very small value, worth less than a penny

fertilizer (fėr′tə•lī•zər) *noun:* Something put on the land to make it produce more and better crops

fragments (frag′ments) *noun:* Broken pieces

frankly (frangk′lē) *adverb:* In a free and open way; not trying to hide anything

freewill (frē′wil′) *adjective:* Done or given by yourself and not because someone tells you to do it

Gabriel (gā′brē•əl) *noun:* The angel sent from God with special announcements

Galileans (gal•ə•lē′ənz) *noun:* People who lived in Galilee

gallows (gal′ōz) *noun:* A frame of two upright posts with a crossbar at the top on which to hang guilty people

Gashmu (gash′mо̄о̄) *noun:* The same person as Geshem

generous (jen′ər•əs) *adjective:* Unselfish; glad to share and give

Geshem (gē′shəm) *noun:* An enemy of Nehemiah and the Jews who were repairing Jerusalem after the captivity; the same name as Gashmu

glorified (glôr′i•fīd) *verb:* Praised, worshiped, and honored

gluttonous (glut′ən•əs) *adjective:* Greedy; eating too

289

much

gracious (grā'shəs) *adjective:* Pleasant and kind

gulf (gulf) *noun:* A wide separation that cannot be crossed

Habakkuk (hə•bak'ək) *noun:* 1. A prophet of the Lord 2. A book of the Old Testament

Haggai (hag'ā•ī) *noun:* 1. A prophet of the Lord who lived when the second temple was built 2. A book of the Old Testament

hail (hāl) *interjection:* A shout of welcome or greeting

Haman (hā'mən) *noun:* An important man in the kingdom of Ahasuerus who was an enemy to the Jews

handmaid (hand'mād) *noun:* A woman servant

hearken (här'kən) *verb:* Listen

Hosea (hō•zē'ä) *noun:* 1. A prophet who lived about the same time as Isaiah and Amos 2. A book of the Old Testament

humble (hum'bəl) *adjective:* Lowly in feeling; not proud

indebted (in•det'əd) *adjective:* Owing money or something else

infirmity (in•fėr'mə•tē) *noun:* Weakness, feebleness, or sickness

inn (in) *noun:* A place where travelers can get meals and a place to sleep

inquire (in•kwīr′) *verb:* Ask questions

insistent (in•sist′ənt) *adjective:* Demanding firmly

insulted (in•sult′əd) *verb:* Treated very rudely or scornfully

interest (in′trest) *noun:* 1. A feeling of wanting to know, see, or do 2. Money paid for the use of money

Jeshua (jesh′ū•ä) *noun:* A priest who went along with Ezra to Jerusalem to help rebuild the temple when Cyrus was king

Jewess (jōō′es) *noun:* A woman of the Jewish people

Joanna (jō•an′ä) *noun:* A woman who was a helper to Jesus

Job (jōb) *noun:* 1. A godly man who suffered 2. A book of the Old Testament

Joel (jō′el) *noun:* 1. A prophet of the Lord 2. A book of the Old Testament

Jonah (jō′nä) *noun:* 1. A prophet who tried to run away from God 2. A book of the Old Testament

justified (jus′ti•fīd) *verb:* Shown to be just and innocent

launch (lônch) *verb:* Push out or set afloat

Lazarus (laz'ə•rus) *noun:* A poor beggar

legion (lē'jən) *noun:* 1. A very large group 2. A Roman army having thousands of soldiers

lo (lō) *interjection:* Look! Behold!

long-suffering (lông'suf•ər•ing) *adjective:* Patient; not quickly angered

lots (lots) *noun:* Objects used for deciding something

Luke (lo͞ok) *noun:* A doctor; the writer of the third book of the New Testament

luxury (luk'shə•rē) *noun:* Unnecessary things for fine, soft, and easy living

majesty (maj'əs•tē) *noun:* Glory and power

Malachi (mal'ə•kī) *noun:* 1. The last prophet of Old Testament times 2. The last book of the Old Testament

Malchus (mal'kəs) *noun:* A servant of the high priest

manger (mān'jər) *noun:* A box or trough in which hay or other food is placed for animals

Medes (mēdz) *noun:* People from the country of Media

Median (mē'dē•ən) *noun:* A person from the country of Media

Mene (mē'nē) "God hath numbered thy kingdom, and finished it."

292

merciful (mėr'si•fəl) *adjective:* Showing kindness instead of punishment

Micah (mī'kä) *noun:* 1. A prophet who told where Jesus would be born 2. A book of the Old Testament

millstone (mil'stōn) *noun:* A large, flat, round stone used to grind grain

Mordecai (môr•dē•kā'ī) *noun:* A Jewish captive in Shushan who was first cousin to Esther

mortgage (môr'gāj) *verb:* To promise to give one's property in payment if one does not pay back borrowed money

mote (mōt) *noun:* A speck of dust

multitude (mul'tə•tōōd) *noun:* A great many

murderous (mėr'dər•əs) *adjective:* Deadly; ready to kill

muscles (mus'əlz) *noun:* Parts of a body that can make the body move

mustard (mus'tərd) *noun:* A plant from which we get a yellow seasoning

myrtle (mėr'təl) *noun:* 1. An evergreen shrub in Europe that has shiny leaves, white flowers, and black berries 2. A low, creeping evergreen vine with blue flowers

Nahum (nā'əm) *noun:* 1. A prophet of the Lord 2. A book of the Old Testament

Nain (nān) *noun:* A city in Galilee

Nehemiah (nē•ə•mī′ä) *noun:* 1. A captive who returned to Jerusalem to be governor 2. A book of the Old Testament

Nineveh (nin′ə•və) *noun:* A great and wicked city far to the east and north of Judah

Noadiah (nō•ə•dī′ä) *noun:* A woman who was an enemy to Nehemiah

nobles (no′bəlz) *noun:* High officers

occupation (ok•ū•pā′shən) *noun:* Business, trade, or work

offended (ə•fend′əd) *verb:* 1. Made angry; hurt the feelings of 2. Caused to sin or turn from the Lord

Ono (ō′nō) *noun:* The name of a valley and plain

organized (ôr′gə•nīzd) *verb:* Put in good order

orphan (ôr′fən) *noun:* A child whose parents are dead

outlandish (out•land′ish) *adjective:* Very strange or queer; foreign

overboard (ō′vər•bôrd) *adverb:* Into the water from a ship

palmerworm (päm′ər•wərm) *noun:* A kind of caterpillar

parable (par′ə•bəl) *noun:* A story used to teach a lesson

294

paradise (par′ə•dīs) *noun:* A happy place for the souls of people after they die

pence (pens) *noun:* Money; coins that were each worth about one day's work

peres (pē′rez) A form of the word *Upharsin*

perish (per′ish) *verb:* To die, decay, or be destroyed

perplexed (pər•plekst′) *adjective:* Puzzled or in doubt about something

persecute (pėr′sə•kūt) *verb:* Treat someone badly because of his beliefs

Persians (pėr′zhənz) *noun:* People from the country of Persia

petition (pə•tish′ən) *noun:* A request made to someone in authority

porters (pôr′tərz) *noun:* 1. Men who are hired to carry burdens 2. Door or gate keepers

possess (pə•zes′) *verb:* To own or have

pound (pound) *noun:* A Greek measurement of money worth about $17 (Sixty pounds made one talent.)

presidents (prez′i•dents) *noun:* The chief officers

prophetess (prof′ət•əs) *noun:* A woman prophet

provinces (prov′in•səz) *noun:* The parts of a country

provoking (prō•vōk′ing) *verb:* Stirring to anger or action

Psalms (sämz) *noun:* A book of the Old Testament written mostly by David and filled with psalms or songs

public (pub′lik) *adjective:* For all people; not private

publicans (pub′li•kənz) *noun:* Tax collectors

published (pub′lisht) *verb:* Made known openly

pulpit (pool′pit) *noun:* A platform from which ministers preach

Purim (pū′rim) *noun:* A holiday of the Jews to celebrate the time when they were saved from Haman's plan to destroy them

raging (rāj′ing) *verb:* Moving in a rough and stormy way

rebellious (rē•bel′yəs) *adjective:* Disobedient and not submissive

rebuild (rē•bild′) *verb:* To build again

rebuked (rē•būkt′) *verb:* Scolded

repay (rē•pā′) *verb:* To give back what is owed

reproach (rē•prōch′) *verb:* To blame or speak evil of

reviving (rē•vīv′ing) *verb:* Coming back to a lively condition

riot (rī′ət) *noun:* Wildness and disorder

royal (roi′əl) *adjective:* Belonging to a king or queen

296

rubbish (rub'ish) *noun:* Trash

Samaria (sə•mar'yə) *noun:* The country between Galilee and Judah

Samaritans (sə•mar'ə•tənz) *noun:* The people who lived in Samaria

Sanballat (san•bal'ət) *noun:* An enemy of Nehemiah and the Jews who were rebuilding Jerusalem

scarlet (skär'let) 1. *noun:* Cloth or clothing that is red   2. *adjective:* Red

scepter (sep'tər) *noun:* A rod carried by a ruler to show authority

scheme (skēm) *noun:* A plan, often an evil or selfish plan

sealed (sēld) *verb:* Marked with a stamp in a way that cannot be changed

severely (sə•vēr•lē) *adverb:* Seriously; harshly

Shushan (shōō'shən) *noun:* 1. The name of a Persian city   2. The king's palace in the city of Shushan

Sidon (sī'dən) *noun:* A city in the country just north of Galilee, also called Zidon

Simeon (sim'ē•ən) *noun:* An old man living at the time Jesus was born

slavery (slā'vər•ē) *noun:* Condition of being owned or ruled by someone else

297

spared (spārd) *verb:* Kept from punishment, harm, or death

spitefully (spīt'fəl•lē) *adverb:* Hatefully; with spite

stature (stach'ər) *noun:* Size; height

steadfast (sted'fast) *adjective:* Firm; not moving or changing

stern (stėrn) *adjective:* Strict or harsh

steward (sto͞o'ərd) *noun:* A man who takes care of the money or things of another

stubborn (stub'ərn) *adjective:* Not willing to submit; hard to manage

stuffy (stuf'ē) *adjective:* Lacking fresh air

submitted (sub•mit'əd) *verb:* Yielded; gave up to another

Susanna (so͞o•zan'ə) *noun:* A woman who was a helper to Jesus

swaddling (swäd'ling) *verb:* Wrapping (Swaddling clothes are strips of cloth wrapped around the body.)

sycamine (sik'ə•mīn) *noun:* A mulberry tree

sycamore (sik'ə•môr) *noun:* A bushy tree that bears small figs

tangled (tang'gəld) *verb:* Twisted around

Tekel (tē'kəl) "Thou art weighed in the balances, and art

298

found wanting."

tempestuous (tem•pes'chōō•us) *adjective:* Wildly stormy

terrified (ter'i•fīd) *adjective:* Very badly frightened

testified (tes'tə•fīd) *verb:* Told as true

tidings (tī'dingz) *noun:* News

tiles (tīlz) *noun:* Thin pieces of baked clay or stone or other material used for covering roofs or making floors

tiling (tīl'ing) *noun:* Tiles; all the tiles in a roof or floor

tithes (tīth̲z) *noun:* One-tenth

Tobiah (tō•bī'ä) *noun:* An enemy of Nehemiah and the Jews who were rebuilding Jerusalem

tombs (tōōmz) *noun:* Cavelike places where dead bodies are buried

trodden (trod'ən) *verb:* Trampled under the feet

Upharsin (ū•fär'sən) "Thy kingdom is divided, and given to the Medes and Persians."

Vashti (vash'tī) *noun:* A Persian queen and wife of Ahasuerus before Esther

violently (vī'ə•lent•lē) *adverb:* Strongly, roughly, or forcefully

visions (vizh'ənz) *noun:* Things seen in dreams or in the mind

299

vomited (vom′it•əd) *verb:* Threw up what was eaten

winebibber (wīn′bib•ər) *noun:* A person who drinks too much wine

woes (wōz) *noun:* Sorrows and griefs

wondrous (wun′drus) *adjective:* Wonderful; marvelous

Zacchaeus (za•kē′əs) *noun:* A publican at Jericho in Jesus' time

Zacharias (zak•ə•rī′əs) *noun:* The husband of Elisabeth and father of John the Baptist

Zechariah (zek•ə•rī′ä) *noun:* 1. A prophet and priest who lived when the second temple was built 2. A book of the Old Testament

Zephaniah (zef•ə•nī′ä) *noun:* 1. A prophet of the Lord 2. A book of the Old Testament

Zerubbabel (ze•rub′ə•bəl) *noun:* A leader of the first group of Jews that returned to Jerusalem

Glossary Words Arranged by Lessons

Unit 4

1
Chebar
Ezekiel
muscles
visions
woes

2
Belshazzar
scarlet
terrified

3
Darius
glorified
majesty
Medes
Median
Mene
Peres
Persians
presidents
royal
Tekel
Upharsin

4
Cyrus
sealed
steadfast

5
endures
Jeshua
public
Zerubbabel

6
Artaxerxes
rebellious
rebuild
riot

7
dunghill
Haggai
Zechariah

8
Ahasuerus
decorations
Esther

Shushan
Vashti

9
account
Haman
Jewess
Mordecai
orphan

10
perish
perplexed
scepter

11
banquet
boasted
gallows
insulted

12
appeased
array
spared

13

petition
provinces
Purim

14

banishment
diligently
Ezra
freewill
porters

15

blush
copper
distressing
reviving
slavery

17

cupbearer
Nehemiah

18

attended
Geshem
organized
Sanballat
Tobiah

19

rubbish

20

amen
interest
mortgage
nobles

21

Gashmu
Noadiah
Ono
prophetess
scheme

22

pulpit

23

booths
Chaldees
distinctly
myrtle

24

affliction
possess
testified

25

dedication

26

arrest
outlandish
tithes

27

cargo
Jonah
lots
Nineveh
occupation
overboard
raging
tempestuous

28

published
stuffy
tangled
vomited

29

Amos
cankerworm
Habakkuk
Hosea
Job
Joel
Malachi
Micah
Nahum
palmerworm
Psalms
sycamore
Zephaniah

30

countenance

dealt
Ephratah

hearken

Unit 5

1

Elisabeth
Gabriel
Luke
Zacharias

2

hail
handmaid
humble

3

Augustus
babe
custom
decree
inn
manger
multitude
Simeon
swaddling
tidings

4

stature
submitted

5

acceptable
brow
Capernaum
Sidon

6

authority
beckoned
launch

7

couch
publicans
tiles
tiling

8

Alphaeus
apostles
reproach

9

bramble
condemn
mote

10

bier
gluttonous
Nain
offended
winebibber

11

frankly
Joanna
parable
pence
Susanna
trodden

12

denied
rebuked
tombs
violently

13

advantage
elders
fragments

303

14
Samaria
Samaritans
severely

15
bandaged
indebted
repay

16
Beelzebub

17
farthings
fertilizer
Galileans

18
ass
bond
infirmity

19
compel

20
bosom
gulf

Lazarus
luxury
steward

21
brimstone
evidence
millstone
mustard
sycamine

22
behold
justified
lo
spitefully

23
stern
Zacchaeus

24
Bethphage

25
audience
devour
persecute

26
absent
betray
converted
deny
inquire

27
agony
council
Malchus

28
Calvary
insistent

29
Arimathaea
centurion
condemnation
paradise
wondrous

30
Emmaus